Southern Recipes & Legends

Southern Recipes & Legends

by Nancy Rhyne

SANDLAPPER PUBLISHING CO., INC.
Orangeburg, South Carolina 29115

First Edition

Published by Sandlapper Publishing Co., Inc.
Orangeburg, South Carolina 29115

Cover photograph of Bonnie Doone
Plantation house by Sid Rhyne.

Library of Congress Cataloging-in-Publication Data

Rhyne, Nancy, 1926–
    Southern recipes and legends / by Nancy Rhyne. — 1st ed.
      p.   cm.
    ISBN 0–87844–133–6 (hardcover). — ISBN 0–87844–134–4 (softcover)
    1. Cookery, American—Southern style.   2. Legends—Southern
States.   3. Southern States—Social life and customs.   I. Title.
TX715.2.S68R48   1996
641.5975—dc20   96-4304
                                                                      CIP

Table of Contents

Author's Notes

Prologue

Appetizers 1

Chicken 7

Beef 14

Pork 19

Seafood 23

BEAUFORT LEGENDS 28

The Twilight Club 29

The Riddle of the Broad River Sphinx 31

The Indian Hill on St. Helena Island 33

Narrative of Sam Polite, Slave on St. Helena Island . 35

The Island that Disappeared 37

Frogmore 39

Vegetables 41

Fruits 50

Casseroles 53

Sauces 62

Sandwiches 65

Soups 67

CHARLESTON LEGENDS 75

Blackbeard's Ultimatum 81

Speculation on Margaret Mitchell 86

The Pirates Who Slipped and Fell 94

Murder on Meeting Street 96

Rebellion 104

Lost at Sea 109

The Daughters Were in the Attic 113

The Murder Trial of Stephen Denaro 116

The House Built for Love 118

Charleston's Secret Millionaires Club 120

Haunted House at 76 Meeting Street 126

*The Day the Press Snitched on Charleston's Most
  Sacred Social Organization* 129

Table of Contents (cont'd.)

Salads 136
Desserts 147
Candies 153
Pies & Puddings 156
Cakes 166
Cookies 180
SAVANNAH LEGENDS 184
  The Ghost of Bonaventure 186
  The Man Who Bought Himself Three Times 193
  Wilmington Island Oyster Roast 198
  Double Bad Luck Day 202
  Black Ankle 206
  Madam Truth 216
  Mrs. Habersham's Terrapin Stew 219
  The Boastful Planter 224
  Where "Jingle Bells" Still Lives 229
  Walking Egypt 234
  The Boat Race 237
Breads 241
Beverages 251
"Canned" Goods 255
Index 260
About the Author 267
About the Cover 268

Two of Aunt Lill's poems are lovingly included among these recipes and tales. See pages 49 and 164.

Author's Notes

Most of my friends collect something. Many of them collect seashells. One accumulates silver sugar spoons. Another has assembled porcelain cups and saucers from numerous countries. My dentist has sunglasses from almost every city that sells souvenirs. Several people have asked me, "Do you collect? Of course, you **must** collect." And it's true. For more than twenty-five years I have collected tales of the South Carolina and Georgia coasts. My husband Sid and I have traveled nearly every back road of that area and talked with residents who told us their narratives. And we visit the Library of Congress each year where we round up other stories. Additionally, I cannot remember when I didn't jot down southern recipes and drop them into a folder. One day I was unable to find a favorite recipe from my years-long collection. After I *finally* located it, I decided to start a "Nancy's Cookbook" in my computer and preserve as many of the collected recipes as I could.

I don't feel that I am *collecting* tales and recipes, however. I really see it more as an act of preserving what is already there. I have accumulated tales that have been passed down through the centuries and recipes that are tried and true over generations, many in my own family. For a long time I've wanted to bring these southern recipes and legends back to life.

On September 1, 1995, I received a letter from Barbara Stone of Sandlapper Publishing, asking if I could combine some favorite tales and recipes in a book. The collection was practically written when I received the letter. Most of the recipes came from my friends, my mother, and my Aunt Lill who was plantation born and bred. Aunt Lill lived her adult life in Washington, D.C., Atlanta (GA), and St. Petersburg (FL), with her husband, Curtis H. Dunn. She enjoyed traveling the world. After returning to her home from each jaunt to some faraway destination, she would ride the train to Charlotte.

Daddy (her brother), my mother, my sister, and I would meet the train and take her for a visit to her family homestead south of Rock Hill, South Carolina. I would snuggle close to her on the back seat and dream of glamorous places, as I fingered her soft fur coat—ever so lightly, so she wouldn't notice—and breathed deeply of the rich perfumes, which I imagined came from deeply carpeted Paris department stores. Granddaddy always welcomed her grandly, and she loved nothing better than cooking for him. Just for fun, she would pluck the name of a city or province from her latest excursion and attach it to her old southern recipes. She always knew how to add a little spice to the lives of those of us who did most of our traveling on foot in our own neighborhood.

I cannot thank Sandlapper Publishing enough for the countless hours its staff spent helping me get this book published.

My husband Sid helped me in millions of ways, not the least of which was testing the recipes we hadn't used in a while—and reminding me at the last minute that I had omitted his decades-long favorite String Bean Casserole. He has always loved to cook. I can't begin to thank him adequately for all he does during the writing of a manuscript and the mad rush that comes after a book is published. I am so grateful to have had him at my side these past forty-five years!

To mention a few of my friends, excellent cooks all, who swapped recipes with me through the years, my thanks go to Marjorie Smith, Camille Dunlap, Miriam Leaphart, Mary Hannah Crenshaw, June Salanda, Twyla Nelson, Tibba Boroughs, and many others whose names should be cited here. And to Pat Callahan, whose column on "The Recipe Page" of *The Sun News* has encouraged me to cook and serve meals instead of always yielding to the temptation to eat out at one of Myrtle Beach's fine restaurants.

I trust you will sample each story and recipe included here and that each sampling will leave a sweet taste in your mouth.

Nancy Rhyne
Myrtle Beach, South Carolina

Prologue

The rice and cotton empire on the South Carolina and Georgia coasts produced for a privileged few a lifestyle possibly unmatched in the history of our nation. That dynasty of wealth and power flourished for more than a century and a half. Except for the robber baron families of the North, the rice planters from Wilmington, North Carolina, to Savannah, Georgia, were the richest people in the land. Their children were taught by tutors brought from England, France, and Germany, while governesses came from New England or Europe. They built fine manor houses, usually of black cypress (heart cypress) and heart yellow pine. Their furniture came from England or was made by artisans on the plantations in popular European styles of the day. Their dining room sideboards held shining silver, along with bone china and fine crystal from England.

Their daughters were expected to continue their education at Charleston and Savannah finishing schools. Sons were sent to military academies, prestigious northern colleges, or revered institutions in England and Europe. From the cradle, daughters were groomed to become wives of planters—mistresses of huge estates—who would direct large numbers of household servants.

It is no wonder, then, that Charleston, Beaufort, and Savannah are renown for both their legendary tales and fine food.

Southern Recipes & Legends

NOTE: Unless otherwise specified in individual recipes, ovens are preheated and baking dishes and stove top pans remain uncovered during cooking.

APPETIZERS

Provincial Meat Balls in Grape Jelly

1 pound ground round beef
1/2 cup saltine cracker crumbs
1/3 cup minced onion
1/4 cup milk
1 egg
1/4 cup parsley flakes
1 teaspoon salt
1/8 teaspoon black pepper
1/3 tablespoon Worcestershire sauce
vegetable oil, for frying
1 12-ounce bottle Hunt's Chili Sauce
1 8-ounce jar grape jelly

Mix together first nine ingredients. Roll into balls and brown in oil in hot skillet on medium heat. Drain; return to pan. Add chili sauce and grape jelly. Simmer 30 minutes. Serve on toothpicks. Serves 4 to 6.

Grape Jelly Meat Balls #2

1 pound hamburger
1 tablespoon cornstarch
1 teaspoon salt
1 egg, slightly beaten
1 tablespoon grated onion
1/4 teaspoon black pepper
1 12-ounce chili sauce
1/2 8-ounce jar grape jelly
vegetable oil for frying

Mix all ingredients together well. Roll into balls the size you desire. Fry over medium heat until brown. Drain on paper towels. Mix chili sauce and jelly together in large saucepan. Bring to boil over medium heat, stirring frequently. Place meat balls—as many as sauce will cover—in pot. Simmer 7 minutes. Serve hot. Serves 6 or more.

Veggie Pizza

CRUST

2 cans dairy crescent rolls

Open and place flat on large cookie sheet. Bake according to directions on can.

SAUCE

3/4 cup Miracle Whip salad dressing
2 8-ounce packages cream cheese
1 package dry ranch dressing mix

Mix ingredients together and spread on crust.

TOPPING

Mix and chop
1 cup cauliflower
1 cup broccoli
1 cup green and red bell pepper
1/2 cup green onions
1/2 cup carrots
1/2 cup grated sharp cheddar cheese

Spread veggies onto sauce and press. Sprinkle with grated cheese. Cut into about 40 squares.

Ham Rolls

1 package party rolls
2 tablespoons butter
1 teaspoon prepared mustard
1 teaspoon mayonnaise
1/2 teaspoon Worcestershire sauce
ham, sliced (1 slice for each roll)

Mix together butter, mustard, mayonnaise, and Worcestershire sauce. Spread on rolls. Place a slice of ham in each roll and heat at 250 degrees for 15 minutes.

Party Mix

1-1/2 cups Cheerios
1-1/2 cup Rice Chex
1-1/2 cup Wheat Chex
2 cups slim pretzel sticks
1 cup skinless roasted salted peanuts
1/2 cup margarine or butter
4 teaspoons Worcestershire sauce
1/2 teaspoon garlic salt
1 teaspoon onion salt
1 teaspoon celery salt

Pour cereals, pretzel sticks, and peanuts into a large roasting pan. Melt butter; stir in seasonings. Pour butter mixture over ingredients in roaster; mix together well. Bake at 300 degrees for about 40 minutes, stirring occasionally. Cool. Store in tightly capped tins. Makes about 3 pints.

Cheese Ball

1 8-ounce package cream cheese
1 package Old English cheese
garlic salt
paprika
1 cup crushed pecans

Let cheeses come to room temperature (about 3 hours). Mix together in bowl or put through food grinder until cheese is mixed thoroughly. Sprinkle with garlic salt to taste. Shape into a ball, sprinkle outside with paprika, and roll in crushed pecans. Chill for 1 hour. Serve with crackers.

Health Cocktail

1 can frozen orange juice, undiluted
1 Red Delicious apple
1 stalk celery
2 tablespoons honey
1 cup crushed ice

Core and chop unpeeled apple. Cut celery in three pieces. Place all ingredients in blender on high for about a minute, until all is perfectly blended. Serve in chilled wine glasses. Makes 4 delicious servings.

Gazpacho

6 large ripe tomatoes, chopped
1/4 cup chopped green pepper
1/4 cup chopped sweet red pepper
2 medium cucumbers, peeled, seeded, and chopped
1 clove garlic, mashed
1 tablespoon lemon juice
2 tablespoons grated carrot
1-1/2 tablespoons finely grated onion
dash cayenne pepper
1/8 teaspoon Tabasco sauce
1/8 teaspoon ground oregano
3 tablespoons bottled French dressing
1/8 teaspoon black pepper
salt to taste

Mix all together. Chill. Garnish with piece of celery. Does not freeze well. Serves 6.

Broiled Grapefruit

2 grapefruit
1/2 cup honey
1 tablespoon apple cider vinegar
Maraschino cherries

Cut grapefruit in half. With a sharp knife, separate fruit from the rind to make eating easier. Mix honey and vinegar. Place a cherry in center of each grapefruit half and drizzle with honey-vinegar mixture. Broil until top is soft and shiny, about 1 minute. Serve immediately. Serves 4.

CHICKEN

Bernard M. Baruch, of Hobcaw Barony Plantation in Georgetown County, South Carolina, ate chicken each day he was in residence at his plantation, according to his nurse, the late Elizabeth Navarro. "Although Mr. Baruch invited many wealthy and famous people to Hobcaw to hunt wild turkey, quail, deer, and duck, he never ate wild game, but enjoyed fried chicken more than anything else," she said.

Honey-Glazed Fried Chicken

1 frying chicken, cut into pieces
1 quart buttermilk
shortening for frying
1 stick butter
1 cup all-purpose flour
1 teaspoon salt
1/2 teaspoon Lawry's seasoned salt
1/2 teaspoon black pepper

Clean chicken; marinate in buttermilk for 45 minutes. Drain. In large, cast-iron skillet, melt butter and enough shortening to rise to half an inch in the pan, to middle of chicken. Put the pieces in a paper bag with the flour and seasonings and shake to coat the chicken. Place chicken in hot shortening (medium heat) and brown, uncovered, on all sides, about 12 minutes. Do not crowd chicken. Turn frequently as it browns.

HONEY GLAZE

1 cup butter
1/2 cup honey
1/2 cup slivered almonds (pecans may be substituted)

In a small saucepan, melt butter over low heat. Blend in honey. Simmer for 20 minutes, stirring occasionally.

Carefully place browned chicken pieces in Pyrex dish. Pour honey glaze over top. Garnish with almonds. Bake at 350 degrees for 15 minutes. Serves 4.

Fried Chicken

**6 deboned chicken breast pieces
buttermilk, enough to soak chicken
1 teaspoon salt, or to taste
1/2 teaspoon black pepper
all-purpose flour for dredging
vegetable oil, enough for frying**

Use mallet to flatten chicken pieces. Place pieces in bowl; cover with buttermilk and marinate at least 2 hours. Drain. Sprinkle with salt and pepper; dredge in flour. Cover bottom of cast-iron skillet with oil; heat to medium hot. Place chicken in hot shortening and fry until crisp and brown, about 12 minutes. Do not crowd chicken pieces. Turn occasionally while frying to evenly brown all sides. Drain on paper towels. Serves 6.

• *This is delicious served on a mound of* Perfect Mashed Potatoes. *NR*

Fried Chicken and Gravy

**1 frying chicken, cut into pieces
1 cup milk
salt and black pepper, to taste
1 cup shortening
1 cup self-rising flour**

Soak chicken in milk for 30 minutes. Drain (saving milk for gravy), sprinkle with salt and pepper, and dredge through flour; let stand 10 minutes. Heat shortening in skillet. Place chicken in hot grease and cook, covered, on high heat until the chicken has browned. (Never crowd the pieces.) Reduce heat to medium or lower and continue cooking 20 to 40 minutes. Turn chicken several times during frying. Serves 4.

GRAVY

Drain all but 2 tablespoons of fat from frying pan. Stir in 1 cup milk and 2 tablespoons flour. Stir over medium heat as mixture thickens. If gravy becomes too thick, add water slowly until it reaches desired thickness.

Plantation Fried Chicken

1/2 cup milk
1 egg, slightly beaten
2 cups all-purpose flour
3 teaspoons garlic salt
2 teaspoons paprika
2 teaspoons freshly ground black pepper
1/2 teaspoon poultry seasoning
1 frying chicken, 2-1/2 to 3 pounds, cut up
shortening

Combine milk and egg in a medium bowl. Mix together flour, garlic salt, paprika, pepper, and poultry seasoning in a paper or plastic bag. Add a few pieces of chicken at a time to the bag and shake to coat. Dip the chicken in the milk and egg mixture, then shake a second time in the flour mixture. Place enough shortening in large iron pan to come one half to 1 inch up the side of the pan when melted. Heat the shortening on medium high. Place chicken in skillet and brown on all sides. Reduce heat to medium low and continue cooking until chicken is tender, about 40 minutes, turning several times. Drain on paper towels. (If using an electric skillet, heat to 365 degrees and brown chicken, then reduce heat to 275 degrees.) Serves 4.

Baked Chicken

1 frying chicken, cut into pieces
1/2 teaspoon salt
1 can cream of mushroom soup, undiluted
1 package stuffing mix
1/2 cup sour cream

Remove skin from chicken. Salt lightly and brush each piece with soup. Reserve remaining soup. Roll chicken in crushed stuffing mix. Place in baking dish, cover, and bake for 30 minutes at 350 degrees. Uncover and continue baking for 45 minutes. Combine remaining soup and sour cream in saucepan and heat, stirring well. Pour mixture on top of baked chicken pieces before serving. Serves 4.

Simply Baked Chicken

1/3 stick margarine
1 frying chicken, cut into pieces
1 can cream of mushroom soup, undiluted
1/2 cup cooking sherry

Grease bottom of casserole or baking dish with margarine. Arrange chicken in dish and pour soup and sherry over chicken. Bake uncovered for about 80 minutes at 400 degrees. If pieces of chicken are small or bony, less baking time may be required. Serves 4.

Barbecued Chicken

2 broilers, halved
1 quart apple cider vinegar
1/2 pound butter
1/2 pound Crisco shortening
1 teaspoon salt
2 tablespoons Worcestershire sauce
1 teaspoon dry mustard
1 teaspoon cayenne pepper
2 tablespoons black pepper

Place chicken on grill. Combine remaining ingredients and baste chicken repeatedly during the entire barbecuing period, more often during the last 30 minutes. Serves 8.

Barbecued Chicken #2

1 small chicken or 6 chicken breasts
juice of 6 lemons
1/2 pound butter
2 tablespoons Worcestershire sauce
3/4 teaspoon cayenne pepper
sugar to taste

Combine last 5 ingredients in a saucepan and heat. Place chicken in a Pyrex dish and baste with sauce. Bake, uncovered, at 225 degrees at least 3 hours. Baste chicken with sauce about every 20 minutes. Serves 6.

Chicken and Beef

4 chicken breasts, boned and cut in half
8 slices bacon
1/4 pound chipped beef
1 can condensed mushroom soup, undiluted
1/2 cup sour cream
paprika

Wrap bacon around each piece of chicken. Line Pyrex dish with chipped beef. Place chicken on top of beef. Mix soup and sour cream and spread over chicken. Sprinkle top with paprika. Bake 2-1/2 hours at 275 degrees. Serves 6.

Chicken and Dumplings

1 frying chicken or 1 hen
2 cups all-purpose flour
salt and pepper, to taste
1/2 cup shortening
ice water

Prepare chicken a day ahead by boiling it in 9 cups water with a little salt, pepper, and butter. Drain, reserving broth. Remove skin and pick chicken from bones. (Cook bones and skin in water for an even better stock.) To prepare dumplings, mix together flour, salt, shortening, and enough ice water to make dough similar to pie crust. Roll out thinly. Cut in small strips, then in one-inch pieces and leave for 24 hours on towel to dry. Bring broth to a boil and drop in dumplings. Cook about 12 minutes. Drain. Place dumplings on plate and top with chicken and broth. Serves 6.

BEEF

Joshua John Ward, master of Brookgreen Plantation in Georgetown County, killed cattle to provide his family and labor force with beef. "Ole Marse Josh send me to woods," said Ben Horry, born into slavery on Brookgreen. "Kill cow. Our Marse treat us right."

Planter's Meat Loaf

1/4 cup shortening
1 onion, minced
1/4 cup chopped green pepper
2 pounds ground chuck beef
1 cup rolled oats, uncooked
1/2 cup catsup
2 eggs, beaten
3/4 cup tomato juice
1 teaspoon salt
1 teaspoon dry mustard
1 teaspoon paprika

Melt shortening in skillet. Add onion and green pepper; fry about 10 minutes. Combine remaining ingredients, except catsup, in a large mixing bowl. Add onion and green pepper and mix thoroughly. Pack mixture into greased loaf pan. Spread top with catsup. Bake at 400 degrees for one hour. Serves 6.

Barbecued Corned Beef

1-1/2 cups water
1/2 cup catsup
1 tablespoon butter
1 teaspoon hot sauce
1 or 2 cans corned beef
juice of 1 lemon

Cut corned beef into small pieces. Mix all ingredients together in a pot and let simmer, covered, for one hour, stirring frequently. Serves 4.

Stuffed Green Peppers

7 large green peppers
1 pound ground chuck
2 tablespoons vegetable oil
4 tablespoons chopped onion
1-1/2 teaspoons salt
1/2 teaspoon cayenne pepper
1 teaspoon finely chopped fresh garlic
1 cup rice, cooked
1 15-ounce can tomato sauce
1 cup grated mozzarella cheese
2 celery stalks, cut diagonally in several strips
1/2 medium onion, coarsely chopped

Cut top off each pepper and remove seeds. Boil peppers for 6 minutes; drain. Heat oil to medium hot in skillet. Brown beef and onions; drain. Add salt, garlic, cayenne pepper, rice, and 1 cup tomato sauce. Fill green peppers with meat mixture and stand peppers in baking dish. Bake, covered, at 350 degrees for 45 minutes. Uncover and continue baking 15 minutes. While peppers are baking, put remaining tomato sauce, celery, and 1/2 onion in skillet to simmer. Before serving, sprinkle stuffed peppers with cheese and spoon on celery/onion pan drippings. Serves 7. [Freezes well.]

Hotsy-Totsy Beef Stew

1 pound boneless beef
flour for dredging
3 to 4 tablespoons vegetable oil
2 teaspoons salt
4 medium onions
4 large carrots, halved
1 cup canned tomatoes or tomato juice
4 large white potatoes, quartered
dash cayenne pepper

Dredge pieces of stew beef in flour to which a little salt and pepper have been added. Using a large skillet, brown meat thoroughly in hot oil until **very** brown. (I almost burn the pieces of meat.) Reduce heat. Add whole onions, carrots, and potatoes. Pour tomatoes over the top. Cover and allow to simmer about 3 hours. Add a dash of cayenne pepper, stir, and continue cooking for an additional hour. (If you don't want the potatoes to cook until they are falling apart, add them at the time you add cayenne pepper.) Serves 6.

Beef Noodle Stroganoff

1/4 cup butter
1/2 cup finely chopped onion
1/2 pound mushrooms, sliced thick
1 pound lean ground beef
1 8-ounce package egg noodles
1 garlic clove, chopped very fine
1 tablespoon all-purpose flour
1 8-ounce can tomato sauce
1 10-1/2-ounce can beef bouillon
1/4 cup burgundy wine
1 teaspoon salt
1/4 teaspoon black pepper
1 cup sour cream
3/4 cup grated Parmesan cheese

Melt butter in large skillet over moderate heat. Add onion and mushrooms; cook until golden. Add beef and continue cooking, stirring constantly, until meat is brown. Add flour, tomato, garlic, wine, bouillon, salt, and pepper; simmer for 10 minutes. Cook noodles as directed on package; drain and wash. Fold sour cream into meat mixture. Butter a 2-quart casserole. Layer noodles and meat mixture, repeating until all ingredients are used. Sprinkle cheese over top and bake uncovered at 375 degrees for 30 minutes. Serves 6.

Spaghetti

2 pounds ground chuck
2 large onions, coarsely chopped
1 cup coarsely chopped green peppers
1 cup coarsely chopped celery
1 clove garlic, minced
2 14-1/2-ounce cans stewed tomatoes
1 12-ounce can tomato paste
1 teaspoon chili powder
1/8 teaspoon cayenne pepper
1-1/2 teaspoons salt
1/2 teaspoon black pepper
parmesan cheese
2 tablespoons vegetable oil

Heat oil on medium high in large skillet. Add chuck and cook until meat falls apart and color changes. Stir frequently. Add onion, garlic, celery, green pepper, black pepper, and salt. Stir until blended. Add tomatoes, tomato sauce, chili powder, and cayenne pepper. Cook for 2 hours over low heat on top of stove. Cook spaghetti according to directions on package. Drain and place on serving dish. Pour sauce on top of spaghetti and sprinkle with parmesan cheese. Makes 2-1/2 quarts.

London Broil

2 tablespoons vegetable oil
1 tablespoon wine vinegar
1 teaspoon salt
1/2 teaspoon black pepper
1 clove garlic, mashed
1/2 medium onion, chopped
1 flank steak, 1-3/4 pounds

Combine oil, vinegar, and seasonings in a shallow glass pan. Brush both sides of steak with mixture and let marinate in pan for 3 hours. Broil steak for 5 minutes. Turn. Brush with marinade and broil another 5 minutes. Slice steak diagonally, as thin as possible. Spoon pan juices over meat. Serves 4.

PORK

"You know, Missy, the kitchen be in that outside-the-house building. That's where I cook the big ole ham. An all-day job, it was. Then I serve it in Hampton house, on a silver tray," said Sue Alston, a daughter of slaves, who lived to the age of 110. Archibald Rutledge referred to Sue as Hampton Plantation's "Guardian Angel."

Saucy Pineapple Pork Chops

1 20-ounce can pineapple slices, drained (save syrup)
3/4 cup cooking sherry
1 can beef broth
2 tablespoons lemon juice
1 green pepper, chopped
1 medium onion, finely chopped
6 large pork chops
1 teaspoon salt
1 teaspoon ground thyme
1/2 cup red currant jelly
1 tablespoon cornstarch
1 tablespoon water

Combine pineapple syrup with sherry, broth, lemon juice, green pepper, and onion. Arrange chops in baking dish. Sprinkle with salt and thyme. Pour syrup mixture over chops and bake, uncovered, in hot oven (425 degrees) 50 minutes. Break up jelly with fork and stir into pan liquid. Turn chops. Bake 10 minutes longer. Combine cornstarch with water; blend into pan liquid. Top each chop with a pineapple slice. Arrange remaining slices around the meat. Continue baking 10 minutes or until chops are tender (when tested with a fork) and pan sauce is thickened. Serves 6.

Spare the Ribs Barbecue

2 pounds spareribs, cut into serving pieces
1/2 tablespoon plus 1 teaspoon salt
2 tablespoons apple cider vinegar
1 cup white vinegar
1 tablespoon sugar
1 tablespoon Worcestershire sauce
1/2 cup catsup
1 garlic clove, minced
1 teaspoon dry mustard
1 teaspoon paprika
1/8 teaspoon black pepper

Place ribs in a skillet and cover with water. Add 1/2 tablespoon salt and 2 tablespoons vinegar. Simmer 45 minutes. To make sauce, combine remaining ingredients in saucepan and heat. Dip ribs in sauce. Grill over charcoal 30 minutes or bake at 375 degrees for 30 minutes. Dip several times during cooking until all sauce is used. Serves 4.

Sweet-Sour Spareribs

6 pounds spareribs
1/2 teaspoon salt
1/4 teaspoon black pepper
1/4 teaspoon garlic salt
1-1/2 cup apple jelly
1/4 cup soy sauce
1/4 cup apple cider vinegar
2 cups tomato juice
3 onions, sliced

Separate ribs. Sprinkle with salt, pepper, and garlic salt. Roast in shallow pan at 350 degrees for 1 hour. Combine remaining ingredients in saucepan; heat until jelly melts. Pour sauce over ribs. Cover ribs and continue roasting 40 minutes. Serves 8.

Glazed Pork Roast

1 5-pound pork loin roast
salt and pepper to taste
2/3 cup brown sugar, firmly packed
2-1/2 teaspoons dry mustard
2 tablespoons cornstarch
2 cups apricot nectar
4 teaspoons apple cider vinegar

Rub roast well with salt and pepper. Place, fat side up, on a rack in an open roasting pan. Bake at 350 degrees. During the roasting, mix sugar, mustard, and cornstarch in a saucepan. Stir in apricot nectar and vinegar. Cook over medium heat, stirring constantly, until thickened. Spread 1/2 cup glaze over the roast; set aside the rest. Continue baking until roast is done. Total baking time is generally 35 minutes per pound. Add some pan drippings to the glaze and spread over roast. Serves 8 to 12, depending on amount of bone in roast.

SEAFOOD

In his last years, Ben Horry made his living by throwing huge oyster roasts for tourists and locals alike. Every fall and winter he poled his skiff through the area's largest salt marsh to reach expansive beds of oysters. The rich bounty of shellfish he plucked from the mud and sold provided the grizzled fisherman with cash. "Mek me livin' now wid de ister. Before, I get seventy-five cents a bushel for ister; now I satisfy wid fifty cents. How I get ister? When tide goes out, I go out in boat wid de tide; tide bring me in wid sometimes ten, sometimes fifteen or twenty bushels. I mek white folks a roast. White folks cum to Uncle Ben frum all ober de country—Florence, Dillon, Mullins—ebery kind ob place. Same price roast for raw; fifty cents a bushel."

As the rice planters had a need for entertainment and fraternization with "their own kind," they formed clubs, such as the Hot and Hot Fish Club of All Saints Parish in Georgetown County. The beginning of that club can be traced prior to the War of 1812. The first clubhouse was on Drunken Jack Island, near Murrells Inlet. On meeting days the members of the club would send a couple of "fish boys" into the ocean in a small boat. When the boat was filled to the brim with fish, the boys would bring the fish to the clubhouse and the fish would be fried by the planters' cooks. While the first course was being served, the fish boys would go back into the ocean and catch another boat load of fish, which were prepared for the second course. The fish were served piping hot, one platter after another, thus the name "Hot and Hot."

Brown Rice and Oysters

1 cup wild brown rice
1/4 cup butter
1 8-ounce can sliced mushrooms
1/4 cup chopped green pepper
1 cup sauterne
2 cups oysters

Cook rice, drain, and set aside. Melt butter. Add mushrooms, pepper, and sauterne to rice and simmer 15 minutes. Spread a layer of rice mixture in Pyrex dish. Dip oysters in melted butter and arrange on top of rice. Continue to add rice and oysters, layer by layer. Bake at 350 degrees for 30 minutes. Serves 4.

Oyster Pie

1 pint oysters
1/4 teaspoon salt
1/8 teaspoon pepper
1/2 stick butter or margarine
1 cup broken Saltine crackers
milk, to cover

In a baking dish, from which the pie is to be served, put a layer of oysters, salt, pepper, and bits of butter. Add a layer of crackers. Repeat layers. Pour milk over and dot with remaining butter. Bake at 325 degrees about 30 minutes. Serve immediately. Serves 6.

Shrimp Creole

1 cup chopped onion
3 teaspoons butter
1/2 cup chopped celery
1 tablespoon all-purpose flour
3 cups water
1 crushed bay leaf
1/2 teaspoon salt
1/4 teaspoon black pepper
1 6-ounce can tomato paste
1 pound shrimp, well-cleaned

In saucepan, brown onion in butter. Add celery and flour, continuing to cook. Stir in water, bay leaf, salt, and black pepper. Turn heat to high and bring to boil. Add tomato paste, blending well. Reduce heat and simmer 30 minutes. Drop in shrimp. Serve hot. Serves 6.

Frogmore Stew

2 gallons water
2 pounds link prok sausage, cut in 1-1/2-inch pieces
2 pounds new potatoes, peeled and cut in quarters
1 large onion, chopped
1 green bell pepper, chopped
3 stalks celery, chopped
3 tablespoons Old Bay seafood seasoning
salt and pepper, to taste
7 ears fresh corn, cut in half
3 pounds fresh shrimp, raw and unpeeled
butter, to garnish
cocktail sauce, to garnish

Bring water to boil in large pot. Put in sausage, potatoes, onion, bell pepper, celery, seafood seasoning, salt, and pepper and boil 12 minutes. Add corn and continue boiling 10 minutes. Add shrimp; boil until they turn pink, no more than 5 minutes. Drain and serve with butter and cocktail sauce. Provide a bucket for each dinner table to accommodate shrimp shells.

Salmon Patties

2 ounces canned salmon, Red Sockeye brand, drained
2 slices toasted bread, crumbled
1 egg, beaten
1/8 teaspoon salt
dash Worcestershire sauce
pinch black pepper
1 teaspoon chopped onion
3 tablespoons vegetable oil

Mix all ingredients together well. Form into patties and fry in shallow oil on medium heat until browned on both sides. Serves 4.

Aunt Lill's
Salmon Saskatchewan

1 1-pound can mild salmon, Red Sockeye brand
1/2 teaspoon prepared mustard
2 envelopes unflavored gelatin
2 teaspoons sugar
1/4 cup cold water
1 10-ounce can mushroom soup
3/4 cup water boiled with 2 chicken bouillon cubes
1 tablespoon lemon juice
1 teaspoon apple cider vinegar
1/4 teaspoon Worcestershire sauce
1/8 teaspoon hot sauce
1 4-ounce jar pimentos
3 hard-boiled eggs, chopped
1/3 cup chopped mushrooms
2 tablespoons mayonnaise
lettuce

Drain, bone, and flake salmon. Stir in mustard and set aside. Mix gelatin with sugar and dissolve in cold water; set aside. Heat mushroom soup to boiling, add water boiled with bouillon cubes. Stir well, and pour over the gelatin. Add lemon juice, vinegar, Worcestershire sauce and hot sauce. Cool. When partly congealed, fold in salmon, pimentos, eggs, mushrooms, and mayonnaise. Pour contents into chilled mold, about 10 inches wide and 4 inches deep. When congealed, turn onto crisp lettuce on salad platter. Makes a colorful and dramatic presentation. Serves 6.

Beaufort

When you first come to Beaufort (pronounced BEW-furt), you will likely try to imagine its colorful past—because all old seacoast towns have them. If you visit the waterfront houses you will see that the rooms are all filled with fine antique furniture, polished to a shine almost every day. If it is winter, fires will be burning in the fireplaces. You will likely dine on shrimp, netted on the trawlers that are always evident on the horizon—or Frogmore Stew, perfected by the people who live on St. Helena Island. You might entertain thoughts of picnics on the banks of the Beaufort River, croquet played on the well-kept lawns, or ghosts moving among fallen ceilings and decay. Mystery is this town's central character—something you'll recognize when you hear these stories.

Laid out as Beaufort Town 1710–11, in accordance with the instructions of the Lords Proprietors, the city is named in honor of the Duke of Beaufort. Six flags have flown successively overhead—those belonging to Spain, France, England, South Carolina, the Confederacy, and the United States of America. This beautiful port city has known the savage war cry of Indians, the invasion of British Red Coats, and the occupancy of the Federal army.

Beaufort, surrounded by picturesque sea islands, is the second oldest town in South Carolina and conceded to be one of the most charming. Its sobriquet, "Beautiful Beaufort by the Sea," is well given. It is only natural that the city's greatest sources of pride are its beauty and its history. . . . *And,* one might add, *its recipes and legends.*

The Twilight Club

The Twilight Club of Beaufort, organized years ago by ferry-boat captain W. P. Roberts, developed into an "anytime" club, and its place of meeting changed from the old ferry dock, which no longer exists, to a wooden railing that ran across a vacant lot on the town's main street.

About 1917, when the Methodist church was under construction, various carpenters, bricklayers, and other workmen on the crew formed the habit of drifting down to the ferry dock in the late afternoon, after their workday ended, to sit and chat with the captain while cooling off. These men were inevitably joined by others, so that by twilight there was quite a gathering. They talked of many things—ships and sealing wax, cabbages and kings—and they dubbed themselves "The Twilight Club."

But, times changed. The Beaufort–Lady's Island Bridge was built, and the need for a ferry came to an end. This daily gathering had become very important to the men of the town, however, and the habit would not be easily surrendered. Captain Roberts stretched a wooden railing across the vacant lot in front of his home on the waterfront, and the Twilight Club began to congregate there. The spot was such a convenient place to assemble, the club members found themselves gathering off and on throughout the day. An errand on the bay was sufficient excuse to stop and join the members already assembled to find out the day's news and gossip. The railing became known as the Buzzard Roost.

To qualify for membership in the Twilight Club, or obtain a seat on the Buzzard Roost, one had only to be white and male. A painted sign hung below the railing stating distinctly that people of color were not allowed. And, although the sign did not state specifically "no women," that was one of the unwritten regulations of the club. . . . *Certainly, no woman was ever seen perched on the Buzzard Roost.*

The lot was eventually sold and plans were developed for the construction of a moving picture theater. Members of the Twilight Club were heartbroken. Progress on the building was slow, however, so the members continued to "roost" there throughout each day and into the night. When one member needed to go to the office to do a little work, his place was immediately taken by a waiting member. Any missing Beaufort husband, sweetheart, son, or father could be located immediately—on the Buzzard Roost, of course—by placing a telephone call to the accommodating café proprietor on the adjoining lot.

The motto adopted by the Twilight Club was "Sufficient unto the day is the evil thereof."

The new theater was finally well underway. With the Buzzard Roost no longer available, the club disbanded. Most of the members are now deceased, and many of today's area residents have never even heard of the Twilight Club.

The Riddle of the Broad River Sphinx

Mention of a Broad River Sphinx occasionally pops up in Beaufort's ancient historical records. It is known that a prosperous planter desired to have his tomb built in the likeness of the great Sphinx at Giza, about eleven miles outside Cairo, Egypt. It is believed that the tomb was built to the planter's specifications—of tabby, with a moat, in the same style as the Egyptian Sphinx, with eyes that stared into the distance beyond the Broad River.

The pyramids and Sphinx of Egypt were erected about 2500 BC as tombs for Egyptian kings. The Great Pyramid, largest of the three at Giza, was built as a resting place for Khufu, the others for Khafu and Menkaure. The Great Pyramid was originally 481 feet high, with each side of its base extending out 761 feet. The middle pyramid measured 472 feet tall and the third 218 feet. Thousands of Egyptians brought tons of material to the site and laboriously stacked the immense blocks of limestone and granite so the pharaohs could then ascend to the stars and the glorious afterlife.

Building the pyramids and Sphinx was obviously difficult work and the job took thirty years to complete. Most of the first ten years were spent moving building materials to the site. Like the slaves of coastal South Carolina rice plantations, the Egyptians were agricultural people and they too worked in the fields only during certain months of the year. The Nile River flooded each July, August, and September, and the Egyptians used that time to work on the great tombs. In coastal South Carolina, the slaves worked in the rice fields adjacent to the rivers from April to early fall. They worked on plantation construction projects during the winter months.

The Sphinx, which measures 240 feet long and about 66 feet wide, is one of the most famous monuments in the world. Its head and body are carved from solid rock, and the paws and legs are made of stone blocks. The face is believed to be a portrait of the pharaoh who built it. No one knows exactly who he was.

Nearly a century ago a strange structure of tabby was found on Riverside Farm about ten miles outside Beaufort. The tabby edifice, which stood on the bank of the Broad River, contained four rooms, unconnected. The walls were three feet thick and seven feet high. There were no doors without or within. Entrance was by an obvious subway. The moat had long been dry. Scholars believed the building was constructed in the early 1700s and probably served as a place of refuge for women and children during Indian wars. Others believed it was the tomb of the prosperous planter who instructed his labor force to build a tabby Sphinx that faced the Broad River. This group further believed that the remains of the planter were somewhere inside the tomb. Tabby remains of a plantation manor house were found in the same vicinity.

At the time the strange structure was found, the farm was owned by Nat Beauregard. Archaeology and romance had little meaning for him and he used the tabby building as a pig pen. His primary interest was in producing "porkers" and his only curiosity in the structure was in figuring out a way to get the animals out of the pens when they were fully grown, since there were no doors. He called the building "The Fort."

The real purpose for the construction of the Broad River Sphinx is not known. It remains a riddle that has never been solved.

The Indian Hill on St. Helena Island

There is a small wooded rise of ground smack in the middle of a cultivated field on St. Helena Island. It could easily have been leveled and prepared for planting along with the rest of the field, but for some reason the plows, throughout the centuries, have skirted it and left it standing there.

St. Helena Island is the largest of the sea islands in Beaufort County. It stretches eighteen miles long and varies in width from four to six miles. The island retains, in a slightly different form, the name of Santa Elena, given by the Spaniards when they landed there on St. Helen's Day in 1525. The name likewise survives in St. Helena Sound and St. Helena Parish.

St. Helena Island was once the home of a number of large plantation owners. When the Federal fleet captured Port Royal Harbor, the planters fled, leaving their beautiful homes and plantations to the mercy of their slaves and the Federal soldiers. Their lands were confiscated and sold for taxes. The new owners later divided the plantations into 10-by-20-acre tracts, which were sold to freedmen and northern speculators.

Before the French and English settled the island and set about building their prosperous plantations and making their fortunes, Native Americans thrived on the land. According to legend, the unusual mound on St. Helena Island dates back to the death of a beloved Indian chief.

When the chief died, his sorrowing people placed his body on the back of his faithful horse and led the horse to the center of the field. The large tribe then began to pass in front of their dead chief, one by one. Each scooped up a handful of dirt and threw it upon the horse and his master. By the time the last member of the tribe had passed, both man and horse were hidden from view in a mountain of sand. Over time grass and underbrush covered the little hill. Today, the mound is home to tall trees and remains green all year.

Narrative of Sam Polite, Slave on St. Helena Island

Wen gun shoot on Bay Point for freedom, I been seventeen year old working slave. I born on B. Fripp Plantation on Saint Helena Island. My father been Sam Polite and my mother been Mol Polite. My father belong to Maussa Marion Fripp and my mother belong to Maussa B. Fripp.

Slaves live on street—two row of houses with two rooms to the house. I had three sisters: Silvy Polite, Rose Polite, and Minda Polite. My father and mother ain't marry. Slave don't marry. Jest live together.

Wen I been little boy, I play in street—shoot marbles and sech thing. Wen horn blow and mornin' star rise, slave have for git up and cook. When day clean, they gone to field. Woman too old for work in field have for stay on street and mind babies. Old mens follow cow. Chillen don't work in field till twelve or thirteen year old. You carry dinner to field in your can and leave it at the heading [end of row].

Wen you knock off work, you can work on your land. You might have two or three tasks of land 'round your cabin what Maussa give you for to plant. You kin have chicken, maybe hawg. You can sell egg and chicken to store and Maussa still buy your hawg. We don't get much fish in slavery 'cause we never have boat. Sometime you can throw out net and ketch shrimp. You can also ketch 'possum and raccoon with your dawg.

On Sat'day night every slave that work get peck of corn and peas, and sometime meat and clabber. You never see any sugar or coffee in slavery. You have straw in your mattress but they give you a blanket. Every year in Christmas month you gets four or five yard cloth 'cording to how big you is. You have to make clothes. You wears that same clothes till next year— winter, summer, Sunday, and every day. You don't get no coat, but they give you shoe. Us never know nothin' 'bout Santa Claus till freedom, but on Christmas Maussa give you meat and syrup and maybe three days without work.

If slave don't do task, he get a lickin' with lash on naked back. Driver give lickin', but Maussa 'most always been there. Sometime maybe you steal hawg or run away to the woods. Can't be no trouble 'tween white folks and slave in slavery time for white folks do as they choose with you. But Maussa good to slave if they done day's task and don't be up to no meanness.

Wat I think 'bout slavery? . . . Slavery done good thing for me, 'cause if he ain't learn me to work, today I wouldn't know how to work.

—from 1937 interview with
Mrs. Chlotilde R. Martin

NOTE:

Today S. E. Polite Drive is a street that turns left from Seaside Road (S-7-77) on St. Helena Island, near Fripp Plantation. Seaside Road extends nearly fourteen miles across St. Helena. As one continues north on this road, marshlands lie on the left side and plantations—such as Frogmore, Fripp, Tombee, Dr. White, and Big House—lie on the right. Many descendants of slaves still live on the island. If one of these individuals is asked where he or she lives, the answer is often the name of one of the plantations, as it would have been when sea island cotton was so plentifully produced there.

The Island that Disappeared

Stories abound about St. Helena and the surrounding sea islands. One of the most interesting is the tale of Egg Bank, once a popular little island off the coast, three or four miles east of Coffin Point Plantation.

The original manor house at Coffin Point, an impressive, three-story clapboard mansion with a red tin roof, still stands today. One may drive two miles along Seaside Road (S-7-77) to the road's end to see the house—or view it at sea from nearly 50 miles away.

The mansion was built by Thomas Astin Coffin between 1780 and 1800. The Coffin family lived on the property until shortly before the Civil War. During the war, the plantation was used by men and women who came to St. Helena to teach at Penn School. Laura Towne, one of the Quaker missionaries who founded the school for black children so in need of education, resided in the mansion. The plantation has had several owners since the Civil War.

If you stand in the yard in front of the Coffin Point house and face the sea, you will view the place where Egg Bank once lay. The small island was a nesting place for thousands of sea birds. Covered with sand dunes, and a few straggling bushes in the center, the island comprised about ten acres at high tide. The spot was well worth visiting during the month of May or in early June when the sand was so covered with eggs and young birds there was scarcely room to step. The birds laid their eggs in the sand and the sun hatched them. As many as fifteen different types of birds could be seen on the island at one time. On occasion, the very sky seemed darkened by the multitude of whirling wings. The noise of their continuous screeching was deafening to the ears. Pelicans did not nest on Egg Bank but chose a smaller island three or four hundred yards away.

At low tide, a long sand bar stretched from St. Helena Island eight to ten miles out to sea and included Egg Bank. Because the island was such a spectacle in May and June, many people longed to view it. Island residents would row visitors to the island in their little boats for a dollar.

Although Egg Bank was once a part of St. Helena Island—at low tide, anyway—the ever-encroaching tides cut it off from the mainland and eventually took it away forever.

Frogmore

Many local residents have referred to Frogmore, a section of St. Helena Island, as the witchcraft capital of the world. They may be right. Witch doctors there have practiced their unconventional medicine for generations.

Traditionally, residents of the area have been extremely superstitious. One local belief is that if one paints the window and door frames of a house blue, evil spirits will not enter the house. People born with a cowl or veil over their faces are supposed to have strange powers—the ability to foretell the future, see things that are lost, etc.

There are certain persons on the island who should be avoided. "Conjurers," as they are known, are dangerous and not to be trifled with. A conjurer can "put bad mout" on people or things (bring them bad luck and keep them from prospering). A spell cast by a conjurer can cause a person to become ill and slowly waste away until he or she dies.

Legend says there was once a woman on the island who gave birth to a child who had two heads, four arms, and four legs. The midwife who delivered the baby fled in terror to a white doctor, convinced that the deformities were the work of a conjurer. The doctor atempted to offer a rational explanation for the unusual birth, but the midwife and her family remained fearful.

Conjure is a very secret thing. Most island natives will not discuss it with outsiders. They will admit quite readily, however, when they have had a run of particularly bad luck, that somebody has "put bad mout" on them.

Frogmore was home to Dr. Buzzard, the most famous witch doctor in the southeast, if not in the entire country. People from everywhere came to St. Helena to be treated by Dr. Buzzard.

The little area of Frogmore is much more than just a home for witch doctors. It is also—probably more importantly—the birthplace of Frogmore Stew, a favorite at some of Charleston's finest restaurants, and a dish that residents of South Carolina's sea islands have enjoyed for more years than anyone can trace. While people in other parts of the South celebrate special occasions with a barbecue or an ordinary fish fry, the citizens of St. Helena Island make a huge pot of Frogmore Stew. Perhaps you'd like to try the recipe for this folk dish at your next family gathering. (See page 26.)

VEGETABLES

Each coastal plantation had a large vegetable garden. "Old Marse Josh see that you get garden," said Ben Horry. "Talk 'bout garden! All run here to Brookgreen to see that garden. That was a garden!

"An English gardener kept all in perfect order and supplied all the vegetables of the season," J. Motte Alston said of his grandfather's Charleston garden. "It was here that I learned my first lessons in gardening, which has ever been a passion with me."

Sherried Acorn Squash

2 acorn squash
salt to taste
4 tablespoons brown sugar
2 teaspoons grated fresh orange peel
4 tablespoons dry sherry
2 tablespoons butter

Cut squash in half and scoop out seeds. Sprinkle each half with salt. Place halves on a greased cookie sheet with cut side down. Bake at 350 degrees for 40 minutes. Turn cut side up and prick inside surface with a fork. Sprinkle each half with 2 tablespoons brown sugar, 1 teaspoon orange peel, and 2 tablespoons sherry. Dot with butter. Bake 10 minutes longer. Serves 4.

Stuffed Squash

4 large yellow squash
2 medium onions, chopped
1 green pepper, chopped
1/2 pound fresh mushrooms, sliced
6 slices bacon, diced
fresh parsley sprigs to garnish

Steam squash until barely tender, about 10 minutes. Sauté onions, green pepper, mushrooms, and bacon together until bacon is browned. Drain off excess grease. Cut squash in half lengthwise. Remove seeds. Carefully remove pulp, leaving a thin shell. Mash pulp and add to onion mixture. Spoon pulp mixture into shells. Place in baking dish. Bake at 350 degrees for 30 minutes. Serves 8.

Double Squash Crunch

3 tablespoons vegetable oil
1 pound onions, cut in pieces
1 pound yellow squash, cut in cubes
1 pound zucchini, cut in cubes
1 teaspoon salt
1 teaspoon sesame seeds, toasted
2 tablespoons soy sauce
1 tablespoon chopped parsley

Sauté onion in oil about 2 minutes. Add yellow squash and zucchini and sauté about 1 minute. (Vegetables should be crunchy.) Remove from heat and add salt and sesame seeds. Just before serving, add soy sauce and sprinkle with parsley. Serves 6.

Red Cabbage Slaw

8 slices bacon, cut in 1-inch pieces
2 tablespoons sugar
2 tablespoons cider vinegar
1/2 teaspoon celery seed
1-1/2 teaspoons salt
1/4 cup water
4 cups shredded red cabbage
2 medium apples, peeled and diced

About 20 minutes before serving time, place bacon in an 11-inch skillet over medium heat and cook until crisp. With slotted spoon, remove bacon from skillet; drain on paper towels; set aside. Discard all but 2 tablespoons bacon fat. Return bacon fat to skillet; stir in sugar, vinegar, celery seed, salt, and water; heat to boiling. Reduce heat, stir in cabbage and apples, and simmer 4 minutes or until heated through, stirring occasionally. Garnish with bacon. Serves 6.

Pickled Beets

1 onion
1 can beets
1/2 cup apple cider vinegar
1 cup sugar

Slice onion thin. Mix all ingredients together in a bowl. Cover and refrigerate for several hours or overnight. Serves 6.

Coastal Orange Carrot Ring

3 pounds carrots
water, enough to cover
3 teaspoons salt
1/2 tablespoon finely minced onion
3 tablespoons melted butter
3 eggs, well beaten
1-1/2 tablespoons all-purpose flour
1/2 cup orange juice
1 tablespoon grated fresh orange rind
1 cup light cream

Pare carrots and slice into 1/2-inch rings. Add to boiling, salted water (using 2 teaspoons salt). Reduce heat, cover, and simmer 30 to 40 minutes or until very tender. Drain. Puree in food mill or force through sieve. (Yield: about 3-1/2 cups.) Combine carrots with remaining ingredients. Pour into well-greased 6-cup ring mold. Place mold in pan with 1/2 inch hot water. Bake at 350 degrees 1 hour or until knife inserted 1 inch from edge comes out clean. After removing from oven, carefully run knife around edge of ring. Let stand 5 minutes before unmolding. Invert on serving platter. Remove mold. Fill center with peas and mushrooms or another vegetable of complimentary color. Serves 12.

Fried Green Tomatoes

1 cup plain cornmeal
1/2 cup all-purpose flour
1 tablespoon sugar
oil for frying
4 or 5 firm green tomatoes, sliced
salt and pepper to taste

Mix cornmeal, flour, and sugar in a shallow bowl. Dredge both sides of the tomato slices firmly in mixture. Add oil to heavy skillet until depth is 1/4 inch; heat over medium high heat. Fry tomatoes, a few at a time, about 2 minutes on each side. When both sides are golden brown, remove and drain on paper towels. Season with salt and pepper. Serve hot. Serves 6.

Hotsy-Totsy
Fried Green Tomatoes

3 firm green tomatoes
1 egg
1/3 cup milk
dash hot pepper sauce
1/2 cup fine dry bread crumbs
1/2 teaspoon salt
1/2 teaspoon freshly ground black pepper
4 to 6 tablespoons unsalted butter

Cut tomatoes into half inch slices. Beat egg, milk, and hot pepper sauce together in a shallow bowl. Combine bread crumbs with salt and pepper. Melt 2 tablespoons of the butter in a large skillet over medium heat. Dredge the tomato slices firmly in the milk mixture, shaking off any excess. Coat with bread crumbs. Fry a few slices at a time until golden, about 2 minutes on each side. Add butter to skillet as needed during frying. Serve hot. Serves 4.

Aunt Lill's
Tomatoes Tivoli

Select large, firm tomatoes. Peel and cut into thick slices. Sprinkle with salt, paprika, and sugar—also, a dash of vinegar and Worcestershire sauce. Dot with butter and cracker crumbs (or bread crumbs) and place under broiler to brown. Serve hot.

"I usually serve broiled tomatoes with my Salmon Saskatchewan for a hot weather luncheon, with green peas, hot rolls, a stuffed pickled peach on lettuce, and a dessert, probably lemon pie or Lemon Lucerne. I had Christine, Daisy and Evelyn in for lunch and bridge yesterday, and that is what I served."
—Mrs. Curtis H. Dunn (Aunt Lill), St. Petersburg, Florida. 1971.

Old South Red Rice

1/4 pound bacon, fried crisp
1/2 medium onion, chopped
1 medium green pepper, chopped
1 cup water
1 8-ounce can tomato sauce
1 teaspoon brown sugar
1/4 teaspoon salt
1 cup uncooked rice

Fry bacon in heavy pan until crisp. Remove bacon and break into pieces. Sauté onions and peppers in the bacon grease; add water, tomato sauce, brown sugar, and salt. Bring to a boil and add the rice. Cover pan, reduce heat, and simmer for 15 minutes. Garnish with crumbled bacon. Serves 7.

Perfect Mashed Potatoes

6 Idaho potatoes
6 tablespoons butter
3/4 cup warmed milk (Do not use cold milk.)
salt and pepper to taste

Peel potatoes and boil them whole until they can be pierced easily with a fork, about 25 minutes. (Don't cut potatoes in half to speed the cooking time.) Drain potatoes; return them to pan and toss over medium heat to evaporate all moisture. Remove from heat and use a potato masher or a very heavy whisk to mash them. Stir in butter, then milk, while continuing to mash the potatoes. Season to taste. Serve immediately, garnished with pats of butter or blanketed with gravy. Serves 8.

Baked Stuffed Potatoes

6 large russet potatoes
1 stick butter
3-1/2 tablespoons grated Parmesan cheese
2 tablespoons finely crumbled cooked bacon
1 tablespoon sour cream
1 tablespoon chopped chives
1 teaspoon salt
1/2 teaspoon black pepper
1/8 teaspoon monosodium glutamate
paprika for garnish

Grease potatoes and bake uncovered on a baking sheet at 400 degrees for 45 minutes. Cut in half lengthwise. Spoon out centers while hot and put in mixing bowl. Save the skins. Add remaining ingredients, except paprika, add to spooned-out potato. Blend with electric mixer for 3 minutes at medium speed. Place mixture in potato skins. Sprinkle lightly with paprika. Brown in hot oven (425 degrees) approximately 4 minutes. Serves 12.

In 1850, Brookgreen Gardens produced 66,000 bushels of sweet potatoes. Today, the South Carolina coast is one of the largest suppliers of sweet potatoes.

Candied Yums

4 large sweet potatoes
1/2 stick butter, softened
2/3 cup sugar
1 teaspoon salt
1 2-ounce package crushed pecans
1 10-ounce package mini marshmallows

Boil potatoes in their skins until done; peel. Combine potatoes, butter, sugar, and salt in a mixing bowl and beat thoroughly. Pour into baking dish and sprinkle top with crushed pecans and marshmallows. Place in 250-degree oven and allow to brown slightly, approximately 10 minutes. Serves 10.

Sweet Potatoes in Orange Cups

4 oranges
1-1/4 pounds sweet potatoes
1 egg, beaten
1/2 cup light cream
2 tablespoons butter
1/2 teaspoon salt
1/16 teaspoon nutmeg
4 marshmallows

Cut stem end off oranges, cutting crosswise. Using paring knife, scoop out pulp. Refrigerate until needed. Scrub and peel potatoes. Cook in boiling salted water, enough to cover, 20 to 25 minutes or until tender. Drain and mash. Add orange pulp and remaining ingredients except marshmallows. Whip until light. Fill orange cups. Garnish with marshmallows. Bake at 350 degrees for 20 minutes. Serves 8.

Fried Sweet Potatoes

**1 sweet potato for each guest
salt and pepper, to taste
butter, for frying**

Peel potatoes and slice thinly. Add enough butter to frying pan to come about half an inch up the side when melted. Fry potato slices at high temperature until they are crisp. Remove from pan and sprinkle with salt and pepper.

• *I emphasize the pepper. NR*

Above the Rain

'Twas a gloomy day, and my spirit was weak
As I stood on the top of a mountain peak.
I looked all around, and I looked far out,
Lost in awe and wonder 'til I heard a voice shout:
"'Tis raining down there–see those clouds just below–
We're above the rain, well now, what do you know!"
Then a thought came to me, sustaining me so:

The idea of one's living above the rain
Has strengthened my spirit again and again.
And now I no longer go under or weep
When the surging waters around me grow deep.
We can rise above troubles, scorns and sneers;
We can lift sturdy hearts above our tears,
And are better for the contest, it oft appears.

–by Lillian M. Dunn ("Aunt Lill")

FRUITS

"*Brookgreen Plantation have ebery kind ob fruit,*" *said Ben Horry.*

"*In the rear of the Miles Brewton House in Charleston is the large garden, extending to Legare Street,*" *said J. Motte Alston.* "[*Here were*] *the broad walks of fine shells from the West Indies, with rows of orange trees on either side, the plots of grass, the huge pear trees from which the fruit could only be secured as it fell on the green sward. . . . A high wall of brick with wide arches protected the entire place, and I must not forget the enormous magnolias in front and the walled fruit, which hung just out of reach of peach-loving children.*"

Baked Apples

Core **apples** but do not peel, except one little strip around the top. Place in baking pan. Fill cavity with **brown sugar**. Dot top with **butter** and sprinkle with **cinnamon**. For extra flavor and color, add some **red candy** cinnamon hearts. Put a tiny bit of **water** in bottom of pan. Bake in microwave on high for 3-1/2 minutes. If apples dry out on bottom, add small amount of boiling water to dish. Prepare one apple for each person being served.

Baked Apples #2

8 medium apples
1/2 cup honey
1/2 cup raisins
1 cup sliced almonds
1/4 teaspoon nutmeg
1/4 teaspoon cinnamon

Core apples. Mix honey, raisins, almonds, nutmeg, and cinnamon. Fill each cavity with the mixture and place in a greased flat baking dish. Bake in conventional oven at 350 degrees for 15 minutes or in microwave on high for 4 minutes. Serves 8.

Pears in Burgundy Sauce

4 firm pears

Peel and core pears, leaving the stems on. Slice across bottom of each so that they sit flat in dish.

SAUCE

1-1/2 cups burgundy wine
1/2 cup water
1/2 lemon, sliced
4 cloves
1 4-inch cinnamon stick
1/3 cup sugar
fresh mint

Combine all ingredients and heat to boiling point over medium heat. Reduce heat, add pears, and simmer for 20 minutes. With a fork, turn pears occasionally to even coloring. Remove pears from pot carefully. Strain liqueur. Return strained liqueur to pot and simmer 10 additional minutes. Set pears in dish, cover with sauce and chill 4 hours. Serve with sprigs of mint. Serves 4.

Baked Fruit

1 6-ounce package dried apricots
1 16-ounce can sliced peaches, drained
1 16-ounce jar Bing cherries with juice
juice and grated rind of 1 orange
1 cup brown sugar

Mix all ingredients together and bake at 300 degrees for 2 hours. Serve with sour cream. Serves 4.

CASSEROLES

Hoppin' John

3 cups black-eyed peas (frozen or canned)
drippings from 4 strips bacon
2 cups rice, uncooked

Cook peas with bacon drippings for one hour, using plenty of water. Add rice and stir. Place in greased casserole dish and cover lightly with foil. Bake at 400 degrees for 30 minutes. Reduce heat to 250 degrees and cook for another hour.

Glorified English Peas

1 15-ounce can tiny green peas
1 2-ounce jar diced pimentos
2 hard-boiled eggs, sliced
1 can cream of mushroom soup, undiluted
1/2 cup sliced green olives
crushed potato chips, to cover

Combine peas, pimentos, eggs, soup, and olives; pour into greased 1-1/2-quart casserole dish. Heat mixture in 325-degree oven until it is bubbling. Remove from oven and sprinkle potato chips on top. Return to oven for about 3 minutes. Serves 4.

String Bean Casserole

3 10-ounce packages frozen French-style green beans
3 cans cream of mushroom soup, undiluted
1 8-ounce can sliced water chestnuts, drained
3 cans (6 cups) fried onion rings

Cook green beans in boiling salted water for 5 minutes. Drain. Place one-third of the beans and one-third of the water chestnuts in a 1-1/2-quart casserole dish. Pour 1 can of soup over the beans and chestnuts, then top with onion rings. Repeat these steps 2 times to form layers. Bake at 350 degrees 30 to 35 minutes or until onion rings are crisp and mixture is hot and bubbly. Serves 6.

Eggplant Casserole

1 eggplant
2 medium onions, sliced
7 medium tomatoes, sliced
3-1/2 teaspoons salt
black pepper, to taste
2 tablespoons butter
1/4 cup evaporated milk
1/4 cups grated cheddar cheese

Peel and slice eggplant. Cover with salted cold water and let stand 30 minutes. Drain well. Sprinkle salt and pepper on eggplant slices. Brown on both sides in butter. Layer eggplant slices, tomatoes, and onions in 1-1/2-quart casserole dish until all ingredients are used. Pour milk over all and bake uncovered at 325 degrees about 45 minutes. Top with grated cheese and bake about 5 minutes longer, until cheese is melted and bubbly. Serves 4.

Zucchini Casserole

1 cup water
1/2 teaspoon salt
2 pounds zucchini, sliced crosswise in half-inch slices
1/4 cup light cream
1 egg, beaten
1/4 cup melted butter
1/2 cup grated Parmesan cheese

Bring salted water to boil; add zucchini, reduce heat, and simmer 10 minutes or until tender. Drain. Place zucchini in 1-1/2-quart greased casserole dish. Combine cream, egg, butter, and 1/4 cup cheese. Pour over zucchini. Sprinkle remaining cheese on top. Bake uncovered at 325 degrees for 25 minutes or until cheese is golden brown. Serves 6.

Tastee Tomato

2-1/2 cups tomatoes, chopped
2 slices stale white bread, diced into 1/2-inch pieces
1/2 cup brown sugar
1/2 cup butter
1/2 teaspoon salt
1/8 teaspoon black pepper

Combine all ingredients in 1-quart baking dish. Bake uncovered at 350 degrees for 15 minutes. Serves 4.

Rice Consommé

1 cup raw white rice
1 can beef consommé
1 can onion soup, undiluted
1 can mushrooms
3/4 stick margarine, melted

Mix all ingredients together in 1-1/2-quart baking dish. Bake uncovered at 350 degrees for about 40 minutes or until liquid is absorbed. Serves 4.

Baked Beans

2 16-ounce cans pork and beans
1/2 cup maple-flavored pancake syrup
1/2 cup catsup
1 teaspoon dry mustard
pinch of cloves, nutmeg, and cinnamon
salt and pepper to taste
3 strips bacon

Place all ingredients, except bacon, in 1-1/2-quart ovenproof dish. Stir until well blended. Place bacon strips on top. Bake uncovered at 325 degrees for 2 hours. Serves 8.

Baked Beans
and Pineapple

2 16-ounce cans pork and beans
1/2 pound bacon, fried crisp and broken into pieces
2 medium onions, finely chopped
1-1/2 teaspoons dry mustard
1 9-ounce can crushed pineapple
1/4 cup chili sauce
salt and freshly ground pepper to taste

Combine beans, bacon, onions, mustard, pineapple, and chili sauce in a 1-1/2-quart casserole dish. Season to taste with salt and pepper. Bake uncovered at 275 degrees for 2 hours. Serves 8.

Baked Beans Wadmalaw

2 16-ounce cans pork and beans
1/3 cup brown sugar
dash hot sauce
2 teaspoons curry powder
1 small onion, chopped
1/2 green pepper, chopped
3 stalks celery, chopped
1/4 20-ounce bottle catsup
1 tablespoon bacon drippings

Mix all ingredients together. Place in 1-1/2-quart casserole dish or bean pot. Cover. Bake at 250 degrees for 3-1/2 hours. Serves 8.

Macaroni Casserole

makes 2 casseroles

1 8-ounce package macaroni noodles
1 pound cheddar cheese, grated
1/4 cup chopped onion
1/4 cup pimentos
1 cup mayonnaise
1 can cream of mushroom soup, undiluted
cracker crumbs

Cook macaroni and drain. Mix all ingredients together. Place in two 1-1/2-quart casserole dishes and top with cracker crumbs. Bake uncovered at 350 degrees until it bubbles, approximately 30 minutes. Serves 8.

Ground Beef Casserole

1 pound ground beef
1 medium onion, chopped
1 1-pound can whole tomatoes
1/2 teaspoon salt
1 10-1/2-ounce can cream of mushroom soup, undiluted
1 green pepper, cut in strips
1/2 8-ounce package egg noodles
1 cup grated cheddar cheese

Brown beef and onion in greased frying pan. Add tomatoes, salt, soup, and pepper; simmer while the noodles are cooking. Add cooked, drained noodles and one half of the cheese to meat mixture. Pour into 2-quart casserole dish. Sprinkle top with remaining cheese. Bake uncovered for 15 minutes at 350 degrees. Serves 6.

Chicken Casserole

2 cups diced stewed chicken
2 quarts chicken stock (saved from stewing chicken)
1/4 cup mayonnaise
2 cups rice, cooked in chicken stock
1/2 teaspoon salt
1 4-ounce can mushrooms
1 cup diced celery
1 tablespoon lemon juice
1 tablespoon finely chopped onion
1/2 cup shredded almonds
1 can cream of chicken soup, undiluted
1 cup corn flake crumbs
2 tablespoons butter

Combine first 11 ingredients and place in a 3-quart casserole dish.
Mix butter with corn flake crumbs; place on top. Bake 30 to 40
minutes at 350 degrees. Serves 8.

Chicken Spaghetti

1 hen, boiled (reserve 2 quarts stock)
6 medium onions, finely chopped or sliced
1/4 stick butter or margarine
2 16-ounce packages thin spaghetti noodles
2 15-ounce cans English peas
1 2-ounce jars pimentos
2 pounds sharp cheese, grated
1/2 teaspoon sugar
1/2 teaspoon salt
1/2 teaspoon cayenne pepper

Cook spaghetti in large pot of boiling water until tender. Drain
and rinse in cold water. Drain again. Fry onions slowly in butter
until clear but not brown; cover and let simmer. Combine spaghetti, onions, diced hen, reserved stock, and remaining ingredients in pot and heat only long enough to melt cheese. Pour into
3-quart casserole dish and bake 20 minutes at 300 degrees.
Freezes well. Serves 10.

Chicken Tetrazzini

1 large hen or 2 whole chicken breasts
1 stalk celery, with tops
1 small onion
1 can cream of mushroom soup, undiluted
1 small jar Old English cheese
1 8-ounce package thin spaghetti noodles
1 4-ounce can mushrooms, drained (save juice)
1 tablespoon Worcestershire sauce
3/4 cup chicken stock
2 cups buttered bread crumbs

Combine chicken, onion, and celery in pot; cover and bring to boil. Add salt and cook until chicken is tender. Drain chicken, saving stock. In saucepan, combine stock, soup, juice from mushrooms, cheese, and Worcestershire sauce. Cook over medium heat until smooth, stirring constantly. Stir in mushrooms. Cook spaghetti as directed on box. Put half the spaghetti in 9-by-12-inch casserole dish, then half the chicken, and then half the sauce. Repeat layers. Top with buttered bread cumbs. Bake 30 minutes at 350 degrees. Serves 8.

Shrimp Crab Casserole

1 pound claw crabmeat
1 medium white potato, cooked and mashed
2 tablespoons apple cider vinegar
1 squirt lemon juice
1 egg
dash Worcestershire sauce
dash Tobasco sauce
1/2 stick butter, melted
1 cup bread crumbs

Mix together first 7 ingredients and half of the butter; place in 2-quart casserole dish. Mix remaining butter and bread crumbs and spread on top. Bake at 350 degrees about 30 minutes. Serves 6.

Crabmeat Casserole

1 5-ounce can sliced water chestnuts
1 cup cream of mushroom soup, undiluted
1/2 cup herb bread stuffing mix
1/2 cup mayonnaise
1 8-ounce can crabmeat

Combine all ingredients in 1-1/2-quart casserole dish and bake uncovered at 350 degrees for 40 minutes. Serves 6.

Coastal Crab Casserole

1/2 stick butter
1 cup chopped onion
1/2 cup chopped green pepper
1 cup chopped celery
3 tablespoons all-purpose flour
2-1/2 cups milk
salt and pepper to taste
1/3 teaspoon dry mustard
1/4 teaspoon cayenne pepper
1 teaspoon Worcestershire sauce
3 eggs, well beaten
2 pounds crabmeat
1/2 cup grated cheese
cracker crumbs

Melt butter; add vegetables and cook for 10 minutes on low heat. Remove vegetables from pan and set aside. Add flour and milk to the pan to make medium white sauce. Cook over low heat until mixture is smooth and bubbly. Add seasonings, eggs, crabmeat, and vegetables to the sauce. Place mixture in greased 9-by-12-inch casserole dish. Top with grated cheese and cracker crumbs. Bake at 325 degrees for 1 hour. Serves 8.

SAUCES

Barbecue Sauce

1/2 cup chopped celery
1 medium onion, chopped
2 tablespoons vegetable oil
2 tablespoons apple cider vinegar
2 tablespoons brown sugar
1/4 cup lemon juice
1 cup catsup
3 tablespoons Worcestershire sauce
1/2 teaspoon prepared mustard
1 cup water
salt and cayenne pepper, to taste

Sauté celery and onion in oil until tender. Add vinegar, brown sugar, lemon juice, catsup, Worcestershire sauce, mustard, water, salt, and pepper. Cover and simmer 30 minutes. Makes 2-1/2 cups. Great on ribs or chicken! Pour over meat and bake uncovered until done.

Simple
Barbecue Sauce

1 stick margarine
1/4 cup lemon juice
1/4 cup apple cider vinegar
1/4 cup Worcestershire sauce
1/4 cup catsup

Mix all ingredients together and heat gently. Do not boil. Makes 1-1/2 cups.

Blender
Béarnaise Sauce

1/2 cup white wine
1/4 cup tarragon vinegar
pinch dried tarragon
1 tablespoon finely chopped shallots
1/4 teaspoon thyme
1/8 teaspoon black pepper
3 egg yolks
1 stick butter, melted

Combine wine, vinegar, tarragon, shallots, thyme, and pepper. Cook over medium heat until mixture is reduced in volume by half. Place egg yolks in blender and beat well. Slowly add butter and continue beating. Blend in wine and vinegar mixture. Place mixture in double boiler and heat until it thickens. Makes 1-1/2 cups.

Blender Hollandaise

1 stick butter
4 egg yolks
1/2 teaspoon salt
1 tablespoon lemon juice
dash Tobasco sauce

Melt butter and heat to bubbling. Place egg yolks in blender with salt, lemon juice, and Tobasco. Buzz blender on and off quickly. Turn blender to high speed and pour bubbling butter in a steady stream until mixture is completely emulsified. Keep warm over hot water. Serve over green vegetables. Makes 1 cup.

SANDWICHES

Vegetable Sandwiches

2 medium tomatoes, peeled and seeded
1 medium green pepper
1 medium onion
1 cucumber, peeled and seeded
1 carrot, grated
1 pint mayonnaise
1 teaspoon salt
1 envelope Knox unflavored gelatin
1/4 cup boiling water

Chop vegetables and mix well with mayonnaise and salt. Dissolve gelatin in water and add to above mixture. Place in refrigerator two days before serving in order for gelatin to set. Makes 16 sandwiches.

Aunt Lill's
Spam Spokane

1 can Spam
1 3-ounce cream cheese
1 tablespoon Smithfield deviled ham
1 tablespoon minced onion
1 cup finely chopped celery
1 cup chopped sweet pickles
2 boiled eggs, chopped
2 tablespoons mayonnaise
1/2 teaspoon prepared mustard

Blend all ingredients together well and spread on sliced toasted bread. Put sandwiches in 350-degree oven for about 10 minutes, or until sandwiches are thoroughly heated. Makes 8 sandwiches.

SOUPS

Turkey Vegetable Soup

2 turkey wings
2 tablespoons all-purpose flour
2 tablespoons water
3 teaspoons salt
1/2 teaspoon pepper
2 teaspoons Worcestershire sauce
2 tablespoons butter
3 cups skim milk
1 cup whipping cream
1/2 medium onion, chopped
1 cup frozen English peas
1 cup diced carrots
1 teaspoon sugar
3 drops yellow food coloring

Cover turkey wings with water in saucepan and cook until meat separates from bone. Remove skin and bones and discard; set turkey aside; reserve liquid. Combine liquid, peas, carrots, and onion; cook vegetables until soft. Add butter and turkey. In a separate saucepan, combine water, Worcestershire sauce, flour, sugar, salt, pepper, and heat over low heat until smooth; fold mixture into turkey and vegetables. Combine milk and cream in a third saucepan and heat to just below boiling; add to turkey mixture. Reheat soup over low heat. Serves 8.

Chicken Soup

1 5-pound chicken, cut up
4 quarts water
3 stalks celery with tops, chopped
3 teaspoons salt
3 tablespoons all-purpose flour
5 medium onions
5 sprigs parsley
1 teaspoon black pepper

Cook chicken in water over medium heat until boiling starts. Add onions, celery, parsley, salt, and pepper. Continue cooking until meat falls from bone. Remove bones. Make a smooth paste with flour and one cup of broth and add to soup. Simmer until thick. Serves 6.

Oyster Stew

2 cups oysters
2 tablespoons all-purpose flour
1-1/2 teaspoon salt
2 tablespoons water
2 teaspoons Worcestershire sauce
2 tablespoons butter or margarine
3 cups milk
1 cup whipping cream

Drain oysters, reserving liquid, and set aside. Combine liquid, flour, salt, water, and Worcestershire sauce in a saucepan; cook over low heat, stirring constantly, until smooth. Add oysters and butter; simmer 7 minutes or until edges of oysters curl. Combine milk and cream in small saucepan and heat to just below boiling. Stir into oyster mixture. Cover and remove from heat; let stand 20 minutes. Reheat over very low heat, if desired. Serves 5.

Tideline Oyster Stew

1 pint half and half
1 15-ounce can New England clam chowder
1 12-ounce can oysters
1/2 stick butter
salt and pepper, to taste
3 drops Tobasco sauce

Combine half and half with clam chowder and set aside. Drain oysters, saving liquid. Melt butter in a saucepan; drop oysters in and cook until their edges begin to curl. Heat chowder mixture. Add salt, pepper, Tobasco, oyster liquid, and oysters and heat to almost boiling. Serves 4.

She Crab Soup

1 10-1/2-ounce can she crab soup, undiluted
1 pound claw crabmeat
1 can tomato soup, undiluted
2 cans cream of mushroom soup, undiluted
1 cup cooking sherry
3 cups milk

Mix together the she crab soup, crabmeat, tomato soup, and cream of mushroom soup; heat thoroughly. Remove from heat. Stir in sherry and milk and return to low heat for just a couple minutes. Serves beautifully in white cups. Serves 15.

Peanut Soup

1/2 stick butter
4 tablespoons minced onion
1 stalk celery, diced
2 tablespoons all-purpose flour
4 cups chicken stock, heated
1/2 pound peanut butter
1-1/2 teaspoons celery salt
1/2 teaspoon salt
1/2 teaspoon lemon juice
1/4 cup ground peanuts

Melt butter in skillet and sauté onion and celery until translucent. Blend in flour. Add chicken stock and cook for 45 minutes. Remove from heat, strain, and add peanut butter, salt, lemon juice, and celery salt. Ladle soup into cups and garnish with ground peanuts. Serves 6.

Jack-O'-Lantern Soup

1 cup pumpkin
1/2 cup chicken stock
1/2 white potato, peeled and diced
1/2 medium onion, chopped
3 tablespoons butter
2 slices bacon, raw and chopped
salt and pepper to taste
1/2 cup water
1/4 teaspoon nutmeg
1 tablespoon cream sherry
1 cup half and half

In a large pot, combine all ingredients except sherry and half and half. Cook over medium heat for 10 minutes. Reduce heat and simmer approximately 25 minutes. Remove from heat. Pour mixture into blender and mix until consistency is smooth. Return to pot and cook on low heat for 10 minutes. Add sherry and half and half. Stir until heated. Serves 5.

Black Bean Chili

2 15-1/2-ounce cans black beans
5 cups canned stewed tomatoes
1 large green pepper
1-1/2 tablespoons vegetable oil
3 medium onions, chopped
2 garlic cloves, crushed
1/2 cup snipped parsley
1 stick butter
2-1/2 pounds coarsely ground beef chuck
1 pound ground lean pork
1/2 cup chili powder
2 teaspoons salt
1/2 teaspoon black pepper
1 teaspoon cumin seed

Combine tomatoes and beans and simmer 5 minutes. Sauté green pepper in oil for 5 minutes; add onion and cook until tender, stirring frequently. Add garlic and parsley to onion and pepper. Melt butter in a large skillet and sauté meats 15 minutes. Add meat and seasonings to the onion mixture; cook 10 minutes over medium heat. Add meat/onion mixture to the beans. Simmer, covered, 1 hour. Simmer uncovered 30 minutes. Serves 8.

Tomato Soup

2 cans tomato sauce
2 cans beef bouillon
5-1/4 cups water
1 quart tomato juice
1/2 teaspoon prepared horseradish
4 drops Tobasco sauce
1-1/2 teaspoons salt
1/4 teaspoon dried basil
12 thin slices lemon

Combine all ingredients except lemon and simmer, uncovered, for 10 minutes. Pour into hot mugs and add a slice of lemon to each. Serves 6.

Tomato Soup #2

1 stick butter
3 chicken bouillon cubes
3 stalks celery, chopped fine
1 small onion, chopped
1/4 cup all-purpose flour
4 1-pound cans whole tomatoes, chopped
3 cups tomato juice
1 5-1/2-ounce can evaporated milk
salt and pepper, to taste

Melt butter in a skillet with bouillon cubes, stirring to combine. Add celery and onions and sauté until tender. Stir in flour. Lower heat and cook for 10 minutes. Add tomatoes, tomato juice, and milk; stir until well mixed. Season with salt and pepper. Serves 12.

Potato Soup

2 cups sliced onions
1/4 cup butter or margarine
1 28-ounce can stewed tomatoes
2 teaspoons sugar
1 teaspoon salt
1/4 teaspoon black pepper
3 cups peeled and cubed potatoes
6 cups boiling water
1 cup half and half

Sauté onions in butter until just tender. Add tomatoes, sugar, salt, and pepper; simmer 15 minutes. Add potatoes and water; simmer 15 minutes. Stir in half and half and allow to heat thoroughly. Serves 6.

Chilled Cucumber Soup

1 tablespoon vegetable oil
1 large onion, sliced thin
7 small cucumbers
1 small onion, finely chopped
1-1/2 cups water
1 teaspoon salt
1/2 teaspoon black pepper
3 tablespoons all-purpose flour
2 tablespoons finely chopped mint
1 pint half and half

Heat oil. Add the large onion, 6 sliced cucumbers, 1/2 cup water, salt, and pepper. Cover and cook until tender. Mix flour with 1 cup water and add to vegetables; cook 10 minutes longer. Remove from heat and blend in blender. Add mint, the small onion, and the remaining cucumber, finely chopped. Chill. Before serving, add half and half. Serve cold. Serves 5.

Charleston

Charleston is built on the end of a narrow peninsula formed by the Ashley and Cooper Rivers, which unite in a broad bay and enter the Atlantic Ocean together about six miles distance. The site was so attractive that the first colonists, who had settled on the west bank of the Ashley River in 1670, moved across the peninsula in 1680.

The Lords Proprietors planned a complex government and an elaborately graded society for the province, which had been granted to them by Charles II. Titles of landgrave and cacique were provided for in the fundamental constitutions drawn up by John Locke, but the scheme was too complicated for a new colony, and the society that formed was instead a much simplified version of that in the mother country.

Charles Town, as it was first called, was settled for the most part by Englishmen who came not only from England, but from the West Indies and New England. Early in its history the city assumed a cosmopolitan atmosphere. The late seventeenth century saw an influx of French Huguenots and French Catholics from Acadia, and the eighteenth century brought Scots and Germans. The nineteenth century saw additional immigration by Germans and Irish. The different creeds of these settlers added variety as well as breadth to the city's spiritual and intellectual life, but its social ideas remained predominantly British. An English gentry, recruited from planters and successful merchants and tradesmen who grew up in the colony, achieved in three generations distinguished standards of education and political leadership.

Architecturally, Charleston retains her eighteenth-century aspect and shares in the excellence of a period marked by good taste and craftsmanship. The architecture bears the character of the best English work of its time, with certain peculiar adaptations necessary in a subtropical climate.

The city of Charleston claims many "firsts," including the *first* independent government established in America.

The *first* time a British flag was replaced by an American flag was in Charleston in 1775.

The *first* cotton exported from America was shipped from Charleston in 1734 to England.

The *first* steam locomotive train ever to operate with passengers and freight was "The Best Friend," which traveled from Charleston to Hamburg, South Carolina, in 1831.

The *first* fireproof construction in America was The Fireproof Building at 100 Meeting Street, designed by Robert Mills. It was occupied in 1822.

The *first* prescription drugstore in America began operation in Charleston in 1780.

The *first* shot of the Civil War was fired from Fort Johnson in Charleston Harbor.

There are many more "firsts" for Charleston and there is no question that this great port city boasts one of the most colorful histories on record. It is not surprising then that many tales have grown up around this magical place. In Charleston, where stories of any kind are valued, they are often decorated—bits and pieces added to make them especially worthy of hearing.

> I can look out one window and see the house where I was born. I can look out another and see where my first South Carolina ancestor owned a plot of land. That was in 1680. But even here [in Charleston] you've got Society *à la carte* and you've got Society *à la mode*. And both of them are a long way from the Blue Plate Special.
>
> —Samuel Gaillard Stoney

It is true that any early Charlestonian exhibited a tremendous satisfaction with his station in life. It has been said that the rest of the world to him was a mere incident—not even the Pearly Gates opened to a city more desirable. Those individuals and families listed in the Blue Books of Newport, New York, and Palm Beach appeared merely an ordinary lot when compared to Charlestonians. The Holy City—as it is known because of its many churches—was dedicated to the principles of English aristocracy, creating a tightly woven world unlike any other in America. Membership could not be gained simply, but rather was based on a combination of lineage, birthright, and land acquired in the right manner. It was a life so splendid and rarefied that even the fantasists of Hollywood have found it unbelievable.

There was little hurry in old Charleston, only a few commercial places of entertainment, an abundance of churches, and an existence where the making of a livelihood was not as important as the art of living itself. It was this reserved, unhurried existence, constrasting so graphically with the noise and bustle of other cosmopolitan cities of its day, which rendered that charm unique to Charleston.

Social life in the colonial city was centered in the home to a degree unheard of in modern America. Inhabitants of the Charleston mansions were catered to by many servants. Each household usually had a housekeeper, a housekeeper's assistant, a mauma, and as many nursery maids as there were children in the house. Each mistress had her maid, a seamstress, and a clearstarcher. The cook had a girl in training and a boy scullion to help her. There were many laundresses. There was a butler and one or more footmen. A gentleman usually had a body servant. And the coachman had under his charge as many grooms and stable boys as the thoroughbred horses demanded.

The one thing, above all others, that confirmed the colonial Charleston citizenry as an institution was rice. There are several versions of a romantic legend concerning the introduction of the grain in South Carolina. The version told most often involves a landgrave, a ship from Madagascar, and a patch of marshland on

Longitude Lane. It is true that the town was the hub of a network of rice plantations, and the plantations were the same age as the town. Thus, the privacy that the plantations provided the town is as sacred to the Charlestonian's soul as his ancestors and his rice.

It has been written that the rice planters were the wealthiest men of their day, except for the established New Englanders like the Rockefellers of New York. One of the most interesting members of this elite South Carolina Low Country group was Plowden C. J. Weston of Georgetown County. When he announced his plans to marry into English aristocracy, his father was not happy, but he consented to journey to England to attend the nuptial ceremonies. When the British bride's pompous father announced his plans to give his daughter 7,000 pounds sterling as a wedding present, the proud elder Weston immediately promised 70,000 pounds sterling, as well as a home in London and another in Geneva.

Rice and respectability were one and the same, and they dwelled together in the cities as they did on the plantations. There was an old saying that Charlestonians were like the Chinese in that they lived on rice and worshipped their ancestors. Considering the amount of rice consumed annually in the Low Country, it also has been said that a dish of rice made all Charlestonians kin.

No Charleston dinner was complete without rice, and Charlestonians were authorities on all methods of cooking it. The favorite style was rice cooked alone, steamed until each grain was separate and firm. It was served with meat gravy or butter. Of the many dishes containing rice, the most popular was "hoppin' john"—rice cooked with small brown field peas and a little pork. And there was the perennial favorite "red rice"—rice cooked with bacon and tomatoes.

Had you dined with an early Charlestonian, you would have recognized the ritual of rice he celebrated daily. Every proper Charleston dinner table held a spoon peculiar to the town. It was of heavy silver, about fourteen inches long and broad in proportion. This spoon was placed on the linen cloth with something of the reverential distinction that the vessel filled with Madeira wine was placed on the sideboard. Take away the rice spoon from Charleston dinner tables, and the meal that followed was not really dinner.

Charlestonians gave many balls. Although the private balls did not compare with the Jockey Club ball, one of the year's most important events to show off the style of the ladies and the power of the men, or the Saint Cecilia balls, always bastions of social privilege, they were nothing to sneeze at.

In 1851 Mrs. Charles Alston, whose husband was a rice planter on the Waccamaw River near Georgetown, made a list of supplies for an upcoming ball that began

> 18 dozn plates—14 dozn knives—28 dozn spoons—6 dozn Wine glasses—As many Champaign glasses as can be collected—4 wild Turkeys—4 hams 2 for sandwiches & 2 for the supper tables, 8 patés—60 partridges—6 pr of Pheasants—6 pr Canvas-back Ducks—5 pr of our wild ducks—8 Charlotte Russes—4 Pyramids 2 of crystalized fruit & 2 of Cocoanut—4 Orange baskets—4 Italian Creams—an immense quantity of bonbons—7 dozn Cocoanut rings—7 dozn Kiss cakes—7 dozn Macaroons—4 moulds of Jelly 4 of Bavarian cream—3 dollarsworth of Celery & lettuce—10 quarts of Oysters—4 cakes of chocolate—coffe—4 small black cakes—

By today's standards, it seems the planters did everything in excess.

A highlight of Charleston balls was Preserve of Fowle.

> Take all manner of fowle and bone them all.
> Into a dove put a strip of bacon.
> Put dove into a well-seasoned quail.
> Place quail into a guinea hen.
> Place guinea hen into the cavity of a wild duck.
> The duck goes into a capon.
> Place the capon into a goose.
> The goose goes into a peacock.

This was roasted, and when served, it was cut, east to west, north to south. The servant sliced across the top.

Besides balls, weddings were performed in the Charleston mansions. Adele Allston was married in her father's house at 51 Meet-

80

ing Street. [This house, now the Nathaniel Russell House, is open to the public.] The wedding ceremony was held in the ballroom on the second floor. Four ceiling-to-floor windows, facing south, opened onto a balcony. Panes of glass on other windows in the room were fitted with mirrors in order to give the illusion of a crowded room. The rosewood furniture was upholstered in blue velvet with pink rosebuds, and the velvet carpet motif was bouquets of pink roses. The mantel was carved in the likeness of dancing women, holding aloft garlands of flowers.

One Charleston bridal reception menu included the following:

Bride's Cake; Groom's Cake
Bridal Palace
Pyramids of Oranges Christalisee
Pyramids of Almonds Christalisee
Tout au Fruit . . . harlequin
Biscuit Glassee . . . Russian Charlotte
Italian Cream . . . Wine Jelly
Maraschino Jelly . . . Orange Jelly with Oranges
Spanish Maringo . . . Blanc Mangee
Spanish Kisses . . . Strawberry Ice Cream
Orange Sherbet . . . Fancy Cake
French Wafers . . . French Bonbon
French Dragee au Liquer
Boned Turkey with truffles . . . Pheasant
Canvas Back Duck . . . Currant Jelly
Capon . . . Grouse
Venison . . . Wild Turkey
Crab meat . . . Oysters stewed
Oyster Patte . . . Gelatine de l'Inde
Chicken Salad a la Mayonaise
Pattie de Fois Gras

—prepared by W. Guillard, successor to A. J. Rutjes

Entertainment followed dinner. There was dancing in the ballroom, usually to the accompaniment of a slave band. One such band might have consisted of a fiddler, a flute player, and a drummer.

Come with me now and take a closer look at this beautiful old city by the sea. Some of my favorite tales of Charleston follow.

Blackbeard's Ultimatum

Kidnapping for ransom was a common practice among pirates in colonial days. Once, however, the notorious Blackbeard captured a group of eminent Charles Towners and demanded a supply of drugs, rather than money, for their release.

On a sunny morning in 1718, loafers on the Charles Town wharf watched with interest the bold approach of a longboat across the harbor. The oars were manned by brawny men, dirty and curiously arrayed in an odd mixture of finest silks and ragged homespuns. Moving rhythmicly on the water, the boat was maneuvered through the waterfront activity and docked. The bowman sprinted ashore, insolently demanding audience with His Excellence, the Governor.

Excited rumor, threat, and plot were rife in Charles Town that day and all that night—for these men bore a message to "Governor Johnson and the Gentlemen of the council" from the infamous Edward Teach, or Blackbeard as he is better known.

The message was unusual and brutal. Blackbeard informed the Governor that he was in need of medicines for his crew and unless the list of drugs presented was delivered immediately to his boat, the heads of Mr. Samuel Wragg, Wragg's son William, and other citizens would be presented to the council. Wragg, a prominent Charles Town merchant, had set sail for England that day with his young son and several companions. Their ship, along with eight others, had been abducted by the pirate just outside the bay.

The Wraggs were a typical South Carolina Low Country family of means and position. The first Wragg family members to immigrate to South Carolina were the brothers Samuel and Joseph. They married sisters, the daughters of Jacques du Bosc, a French Huguenot immigrant who had become a merchant in Charles Town.

Samuel Wragg had landed in the province by March 6, 1710, for on that day he delivered to the Council a letter from the Lords

Charleston

Proprietors. In 1712 he became a member of the Provincial House of Commons, and in 1717 a member of the Council. On that fateful day in 1718, outward bound from Charles Town to England, the vessel in which Wragg traveled was commandeered by Blackbeard just off the Charles Town bar. That was a year when the Crown was anointing certain brave Englishmen with the responsibility of suppressing piracy in the West Indies. Capt. Woodes Rogers, governor of the Bahamas, believed piracy to be shameful and he desired an end to the epic drama. The pirates, once bona fide English fleet personnel, now out of naval service, were desperate men. They were offspring of Continental hostilities, religious wars, and England's refuse population, which had been dumped on her West Indian islands. Periods of widespread pirate activity were usually related to times of intense commercial rivalry or bitter religious hostility among the great nations.

Upon seeing a sloop turn out of a bay, the pirates would hoist a flag of colors and pull alongside the vessel. Once securely positioned, they would haul down the flag, hoist their black flag, fire a broadside, and board the sloop. Blackbeard was the most feared of all the sea's marauders.

The infamous pirate's name was given him because of his particularly luxuriant beard. It was exceptional in length and grew close under his eyes. He enhanced it with ribbons that resembled small tails. For even greater effect, matches were stuck under his hat, and when they were ignited, each side of his face lit up, giving his eyes an unnatural and wild appearance. In times of action he wore a sling over his shoulders, in which he carried three brace of pistols hung in holsters.

The Carolina prisoners were taken aboard Blackbeard's ship after being mercilessly questioned concerning the lading of their vessels and the number and worth of other traders in the harbor. The prisoners were threatened death for lying or evading answers. The child, William Wragg, was treated as roughly as the adults and locked away below the deck with the others. They all watched as the hatch slammed shut upon them.

The prisoners were told about the extraordinary circumstances surrounding their capture and promised they would be held prisoner only until a general council was held and the pirates' demands were met. Blackbeard and his crew were in need of medicines and these had to be supplied from the province. He was sending a list of the needed drugs to the Governor and Council, and when the ransom was received, he would determine how well the demand had been complied with. If the Governor and Council did not respond to all demands, selected prisoners would be sacrificed.

Samuel Wragg boldly suggested to his captor that the Governor might not be able to comply with every part of the request. Certain drugs might not be available in the province. He offered to go into Charles Town in order to induce the Governor and Council to act on the request. Wragg pointed out that his son's remaining onboard would assure his return, for he would never desert William to the hands of a pirate. Blackbeard would not agree to the offer. He realized that Wragg was a prominent and valued citizen in the town and he would be risking the loss of his most important bargaining chip. After some debate, however, he selected several others for the task and they were set off from the fleet in a canoe. There was nothing to do then but wait.

When some time had passed and the prisoners had not returned, Blackbeard determined they had deceived him. He had Wragg hauled before him. Wragg, believing something dreadful must have happened to the canoe, begged for just one more day—only one day. Blackbeard agreed.

Another day passed and still nothing was heard. Blackbeard was furious. No man onboard that day would have bet a pound sterling on his life. As Blackbeard looked through his spyglass, a small boat suddenly came into view. But, alas, it was not the boat longed for—only a courier bearing the tale that the canoe had been blown off course by a sudden squall.

All provisions and goods were immediately removed from the prisoners' ships. When the prisoners, all gentlemen of rank, realized what was happening, they became terrified, believing that the next step must certainly be death for them all. As the pirates continued to empty their ships, the prisoners speculated on the way in which they would be disposed of. Some believed a match would torch each ship. Others believed their vessels would be sunk. Each person seemed destined for sacrifice.

Blackbeard's ferocity, Governor Johnson knew, was beyond question, and he was at a loss as to what to do. The Council was divided on whether to allow the indignity. The powerful friends and family of Wragg, however, demanded that the life of so valued a citizen not be sacrificed for the sake of a few drugs and the scruples of men.

The crew of the longboat, who had been sent to urge support of the Governor and secure the needed medicines, sat uneasily in a public tavern amusing themselves with the colony's food and rum while they awaited the Council's decision. Citizens of Charles Town, fearing that reprisals would be made against Wragg, contented themselves with black looks and bombardments of uncomplimentary remarks.

Governor Johnson, mindful that the Proprietors had been repeatedly urged to send a frigate for defense of commerce, decided to protect the lives of the captured citizens and meet Blackbeard's demands.

In the meantime, back onboard the pirate ship, the prisoners had grown more and more afraid, believing every moment to be their last. Finally, their prayers were answered.

The longboat returned, and a chest of drugs was brought on deck. Blackbeard in turn released his terrified captives, but not before he had stripped them of all their possessions, including the $6,000 carried by the wealthy Samuel Wragg. When the party of prisoners set out for shore, they were practically naked.

The dreaded Blackbeard—his ship filled with the loot of many a plundered vessel, his medicine chest stocked with drugs for the ill and wounded—sailed on in his desperate course.

William Wragg, the eldest son of Samuel Wragg, who as a child had been captured by Blackbeard along with his father, grew to be a man of ability, fortune, and the highest character. He was offered the post of Chief Justice of the Colony and declined it. He served as a member of the Council, but his staunch loyalty to the Crown caused his expulsion in 1777 from his native land. On his voyage to England he drowned in a shipwreck off the coast of Holland. A memorial stands today in his honor in Westminster Abbey.

Speculation on Margaret Mitchell

Margaret came to Charleston and did exhaustive research. She interviewed Samuel Gaillard Stoney, architect, arbiter in the gentle Southern tradition and head of the South Carolina Historical Society; Milby Burton, director of the Charleston Museum; and me. She must have used certain names, mannerisms, and so forth from her research for her book *Gone with the Wind*, the most famous novel in the English speaking world and the most famous film of all time. Of course Margaret used mannerisms. Copying mannerisms is the reason why there is no objective reporting. Margaret Mitchell learned just what Charlestonians accepted and what they did not accept.

Rhett Butler was a Charlestonian and undoubtedly he came from a fine family. Being a blockade runner made him a hero in the Confederacy. All ports were blockaded. The only way the South could get medical and military supplies was by blockade. The goods came from Bermuda, Nassau, and England.

Rhett Butler was 'Old Charleston.' He was an adventurer, patterned after the younger sons who had to make their own living, but Rhett Butler never wanted to be one of them. Margaret Mitchell created him that way. He would have been accepted by Old Charleston, but he never wanted to be one of them.

—from a telephone interview
with Jack Leland,
former managing editor of
Charleston *Post & Courier*
September 9, 1992

THE TIME: Late 1920s
THE PLACE: Charleston

Margaret Mitchell has just come to town. The locals are spreading the word that she is writing a Civil War novel.

Mitchell receives a call from a news reporter. "You doing research for your novel?"

"I'm here to decide upon a name for my hero," answers Mitchell, with a 'secret agent' attitude.

Mitchell went on to speak in melodic southern cadences, but her silences spoke too. She was not one to gush "Yes, a fine old Charleston name!" or "Don't you adore Charleston family titles?" but rather someone who took a deep breath, thought about what she wanted to say, and expressed herself in complete thoughts. "I want a one-syllable, South Carolina first name for the hero in my novel. He is a blockade runner, and as there was no blockade running in Georgia, I'm making him a Charlestonian."

"And for a last name?"

"Something widely known and famous on the Georgia coast. A two-syllable last name that will identify, specify, or designate a southern family."

"There are many family names to choose from," the reporter pointed out.

"As fairy-tale-like as this project sounds, there are tremendous limitations on names. It is important that you write in your newspaper article that I do not wish to embarrass anyone. The name will be unique. I will make it up."

According to the newspaper reporter, Mitchell was more than driven to bring a realness to the novel by composing the perfect name. She displayed a sort of hunger as she searched, pondering over documents in several libraries and at the Charleston Historical Society.

There is no question that Mitchell's attention was drawn to the numerous files on Col. William Rhett, who lay at rest in a vault in St. Philip's churchyard. Colonel Rhett led the party that captured Stede Bonnet, thus putting an end to piracy in Charleston's waters.

Rhett's home at 54 Hasell Street was one of the city's oldest residences, and it had endured. Mitchell's hero, like Colonel Rhett, had
a connection with a pirate.

In November 1694 William Rhett arrived in Carolina. He was
twenty-eight years old. His name had been changed from Rait or
Rhet in order to meet English standards of spelling. A man of culture and education, Rhett was captain of and owned a half-interest
in the frigate *Providence*, which had begun the voyage in London,
stopped in Gambo, Africa, and continued to Charles Town. Rhett
was married to the former Sarah Cooke. They had a daughter,
Christiana.

Although Rhett's education and training was entirely naval, he
possessed the kind of spirit that made good commanders on land as
well as upon the sea. Gov. Nathaniel Johnson believed Rhett's lack
of technical knowledge was of small account under the conditions
then prevailing in Carolina and appointed him to the command of
the colonial militia. Although Rhett's services rendered at sea would
later bring him the rank of vice admiral, he was more pleased with
the distinction of being appointed colonel by the governor.

Colonel Rhett led several expeditions that succeeded without
bloodshed, and dozens of prisoners were brought into the port of
Charles Town. By 1718 there were said to be fifteen hundred free-
booters terrorizing the American coast. The pirates were so daring
and troublesome they blockaded the port of Charles Town and alternately slipped into the inlets of the Cape Fear River for supplies.
By this time the governor of South Carolina was Robert Johnson,
son of the man who had given Rhett his commission. This governor
fitted out two armed sloops and gave command of them to Colonel
Rhett.

Rhett had not proceeded far into the harbor before running into
trouble. Just off the bar sat a pirate ship, plundering vessels as they
entered and left the harbor. This particular pirate ship was commanded by Stede Bonnet, a retired British officer who had joined
the ranks of piracy. Bonnet was the first to force his prisoners to
walk the plank to their deaths as punishment. Many people were
astonished at Bonnet's new chosen profession. He was a retired major

from Barbados—a wealthy man of good education. His unhappy marriage was blamed for his change of heart—and vocation. He had left his old life behind and slipped away with a sloop of ten guns manned by seventy outlaws. Regardless of the reason for his becoming a pirate, Stede Bonnet was one, and, on this day, he fled to the Cape Fear River with Rhett in pursuit.

All that day and into the night the two captains played cat and mouse, as both sides prepared for battle. Rhett's ship the *Henry* had eight guns and seventy men, and his *Sea Nymph* had eight guns and sixty men. Bonnet sailed the *Royal James*. The two men were ignorant of the approaching shoals, and all three vessels ran aground. There was a battle at pistol range. As the battled raged, the *Henry* suffered casualties. It became clear that victory would come to the ship favored by the next high tide.

Rhett was the lucky one. The rising tide gave his ship the advantage. When Bonnet saw the Colonel preparing to board the *Royal James*, he ran up the white flag. On October 3, 1718, Colonel Rhett sailed the pirate ship into Charles Town harbor with Bonnet and his crew as prisoners. The two ships that Bonnet had previously captured were brought in behind. Bonnet's crew was held in the watchhouse under heavy military guard, but their infamous leader was kept at the residence of Capt. Nathaniel Partridge, provost marshal of the colony.

A trial was scheduled for October 28, but a guard was bribed and Bonnet and David Herriot, his sailing master, escaped. Bonnet was recaptured by Rhett, after an exchange of gunfire that killed Herriot.

Bonnet's crew was tried, and twenty-nine of them were hanged on November 8. Their bodies were left *dancing* for several days as an example to those sympathetic to the act of piracy. They were then buried below the high water mark off White Point. Stede Bonnet was tried two days later, and Chief Justice Trott set his date for execution as December 10.

On the appointed day, Bonnet was dragged in a hurdle to the place of execution, near where his men had died. He arrived in shackles, clutching a bouquet of fall blossoms. The governor had been pressured to pardon him, as people felt sympathy for the educated, dashing *gentleman* who had been driven to freebooting by a nagging wife. But the governor's mind was made up. On December 10, 1718, the executioner dropped the noose over his head and around his neck, and Bonnet was *swung off* the cart. It must have been an agonizing death. Stede Bonnet too was buried off White Point.

Rhett and his wife Sarah had six more children: five daughters and a son. One of the children was born in Sarah's fiftieth year. Only four of the children lived to maturity. All married well. Daughters Sarah and Catharine married prosperous planters on the Cape Fear River in North Carolina. Catharine's husband owned what is today Orton Plantation, near Wilmington. Daughter Mary married Richard Wright, son of Chief Justice Robert Wright and brother of Sir James Wright, the last colonial governor of Georgia. William married his first cousin Mary Trott, the only child of Chief Justice Nicholas Trott. William died at age thirty-three, leaving no son to bear his name.

One might wonder what reward was given to the brave Colonel Rhett. He rose higher than ever in favor and influence. He was apppointed Collector of the Port and Governor of the Bahamas. Before he could assume the governorship he died on January 12, 1722, at the age of fifty-seven.

Historians have described Rhett as a man of decided courage and conduct. South Carolina's archives describe Rhett as "a man of dauntless courage, tremendous energy and great political sagacity," "a man possessed of a high temper," and "a man who resorted to extreme measures, without hesitation, to accomplish his purposes." Likely, Rhett's highest tribute came from Governor Nicholson, one of his enemies. Immediately after the colonel's death, Nicholson wrote to the Lords Proprietors urging them to send to America as quickly as possible a successor for Colonel Rhett, adding, "I am afraid there are not many persons here qualified to succeed Rhett."

The people of South Carolina today continue to hold the name Rhett in high esteem. This regard is warranted. Col. William Rhett played a major role in American history by bringing piracy off the coast of South Carolina to a close. Thanks to Margaret Mitchell, through her fictional history, the name Rhett is known and regarded across the entire nation and throughout other parts of the world.

While deciding on the two-syllable Georgia coast surname for her hero, Mitchell must have already considered Butler. About five years prior to her Charleston visit, where she read "hundreds and hundreds" of pages of history in order to decide on a one-syllable South Carolina first name for her character, she had written an essay for an Atlanta newspaper on the Butlers of South Carolina and Georgia.

Pierce Butler was the first United States senator to be elected from South Carolina. He was born at Ballintemple, County Carlow, Ireland, July 11, 1744, the third son of Sir Richard Butler, the fifth Baronet of Cloughrenan. The Butlers claimed descent from the great Butler family, who produced the dukes and marquises of Ormonde. Pierce Butler's mother was Henrietta Percy, daughter of Anthony Percy, the Mayor of Dublin, whose family claimed the Dukedom of Northumberland unsuccessfully. Pierce Butler had a commission in the British army purchased for him when he was eleven years old, and he saw active service against the French in Canada while in his teens.

Butler came to America in 1765 as a major in the Twenty-ninth British Regiment. In 1771 he married Mary "Polly" Middleton, a member of one of South Carolina's most prestigious families. Butler then retired from the army and began his life as a plantation master.

During his tenure as senator, Butler lived in Philadelphia, but spent some time in coastal Georgia, where he owned three large tracts of land. Despite the significant contribution Butler made as senator to the development of South Carolina and, consequently, the nation, he was all but forgotten in the state.

In his later years, his greatest wish was that the family name be carried on. After his death in 1822, his will directed that his Georgia property pass to any of his grandsons—the children of his daughter Sarah and her husband Dr. James Mease—with the stipulation that whichever of the boys wanted to be his heir had to change his last name to Butler. One grandson died in boyhood. Another, John, favored retaining the name Mease. But fifteen-year-old Butler Mease legally took the name Pierce Butler, II, and inherited the property. Years later, John decided to change his name as well, and Pierce conveyed to him half the Georgia property. Although Pierce Butler, II, became a prosperous planter, his reputation was largely due to his marrying Fanny Kemble.

Frances Anne "Fanny" Kemble was a noted English actress when she arrived in the United States in 1832 to tour the country with her father. Immensely popular, she was accepted into the high society of all cities she visited. But it was Pierce Butler who won her heart. After their marriage in 1834, Fanny retired from the stage.

Fanny was interested in seeing the plantation and the slaves who worked the large tracts. In 1838, when Pierce planned a business trip to take a look at his property, Fanny accompanied him, along with their two children: Sarah, aged three, and Frances, aged six months.

Fanny asked a friend, Elizabeth Dwight Sedgewick, to join them on their trip to Georgia. Elizabeth was unable to accompany them, so Fanny kept a journal of what she witnessed, planning to present the book to her friend. Sadly, Fanny didn't like much of what she witnessed.

By the time the Civil War broke out, Fanny was hearing ever increasing expressions of sympathy for the Confederacy and defenses of the institution of slavery. She became determined to publish her journal to show slavery in a true light. Her *Journal of a Residence on a Georgian Plantation, 1838–39* was published in England in May 1863. A few months later, it was published in America by Harper Brothers. Needless to say, it caused great controversy. A classic work, it remains in print today.

Margaret Mitchell found Pierce and Fanny Butler interesting, to say the least, and her Atlanta newspaper essay on them brought attention to her writing. It is not surprising that the two-syllable Georgia coast name she chose for her hero was Butler.

Most would agree that Margaret Mitchell selected the perfect name for her hero. Certainly the name Rhett Butler will live on and on. Unfortunately the name she selected for her novel's heroine was not as successful. While writing *Gone with the Wind*, Mitchell called her heroine Daisy. The name was obviously changed before publication.

The Pirates Who Slipped and Fell

Wealthy Charles Town merchants regularly sailed to London and loaded their vessels with valuables from the East India Company. Pirates knew of this practice and were invariably lying in wait as the merchant ships entered the Charles Town harbor on their return. These piracies had become a subject of serious consideration in mother England, engaging the earnest attention of the government.

Robert Daniell (1646–1718) was governor of South Carolina under the Lords Proprietors in 1716 and 1717. His son John owned one of the merchant ships that ran back and forth to London bringing needed supplies to the colony. John was young and brave—and well aware of the pirates in the port. He knew the risk of losing both the merchandise and his ship, as the pirates often sank the merchant vessels after emptying them.

On one return voyage, as he set his sights on the Charles Town harbor, Captain Daniell saw a pirate ship moving toward him. The wind was in the pirate's favor and Daniell knew he would be overtaken before he could reach port. He had little time to form a strategy, as the black flag was being hoisted and the vessel continuing to draw near.

Looking about him for inspiration, Daniell was suddenly struck by the fact that his crew wore no shoes. He believed the pirates were also barefoot. He yelled at his crew to beat up glass and scatter it about the deck. Demijohns of water and wine were smashed and thrown this way and that. The deck was not only covered in broken glass. It was also wet and slick.

Captain Daniell and his crew offered no resistance as the pirates climbed onboard their ship. As each freebooter stepped on deck, he fell pell-mell—sending his cutlass, poleax, or pistol sliding out of his reach. It was true: the pirates were barefoot. The merciless men had no way to protect themselves. Many leaped overboard and swam for shore, but Daniell was quick to respond, ordering a canoe manned and sent in pursuit of them.

The pirates who had slid across the wooden deck and fallen on sharp spikes of glass were growing weak and faint as a result of their bleeding wounds. Realizing escape was impossible, one begged in the most earnest manner that he be given quarter.

Some of the men were taken prisoner. Others, who displayed a fondness for violence, were thrown into the sea. Many were left lying on the deck, moaning.

When the thieves were all disposed of, Daniell seized possession of the pirate ship and helped himself to its cargo, which consisted of many valuable items and a hoard of money.

Daniell returned to Charleston with his capture and remained in the city to ponder his situation. Finally, he made his decision. He sold his merchant vessel and the pirate ship and bought a large plantation in North Carolina. Having no knowledge of agriculture, he hired an overseer. The plantation was a success and Daniell lived there the rest of his life.

Murder on Meeting Street

On November 1, 1933, a baffling *murder* took place in Charleston, involving one of the city's most prominent women. The circumstances surrounding the event were so strange, for years there was disagreement about whether it actually *was* a murder.

Here is the story, reader. You decide.

On that November evening aforementioned, Mrs. John Ravenel was returning to her home on Tradd Street from a dinner with friends at the Fort Sumter Hotel. Mary Ravenel, like other Charlestonians, enjoyed "genteel entertainment," which in the historic port city usually consisted of an elegantly served meal followed by spicy conversation. No one, it is told, could spice a conversation quite so flavorfully as Mrs. Ravenel.

Many years before, as a young woman, Miss Mary Mack of Detroit had married William Martin, the owner of several plantations in the vicinity of Savannah. William Martin died in 1903, leaving Mary with four children to raise alone. Her second marriage three years later was more fortunate. John Ravenel, a son of St. Julien Ravenel, was a man of "the quality." St. Julien had studied medicine in Philadelphia and France and he ran a successful medical practice. He also owned a large plantation called Stony Landing on which he had developed the first limestone mining operation in the state. John was a prominent businessman. Mary's origins were of scant social importance once she married into the illustrious Ravenel family.

Mary especially loved the Ravenel mansion on East Battery—as did everyone else. Even women in magnificent clothing and jewels visiting from Paris ordered their drivers to slow the automobiles as they passed by in order to get a better glimpse of the house. The twenty-four rooms, five halls, six baths, and four stairways were spectacular. Walls were thirty-two inches thick, and recessed paneling and a high chair rail decorated the second-floor drawing room, which offered a grand view of the harbor. The home had seven black marble mantels.

The marriage to John was a good one for Mary, although he preceded her in death by many years. After his death, she moved into the smaller house on Tradd Street, where she entertained often.

No doubt Mary had her good qualities. She was active in her church and in the community, and she was said to be loyal and devoted to her friends. But, she also had a wicked tongue, often employed in gossip.

One of Mary's favorite topics of conversation was "that man, the photographer" who lived at the corner of Meeting Street and Price's Alley. So frequently had he been maligned by Mrs. Ravenel as she gorged herself with Low Country foods at these dinners, word of the idle rumors reached the ear of the photographer, Mr. Payne. This "leak" didn't slow the tittle-tattle of Mrs. Ravenel, however. After dinner, or over a bridge table, she buzzed the latest scandal of the port city.

Since Mrs. Ravenel lived in the historic section of Charleston with the other blue bloods, she was part of the city's highest social stratum. Although some members of the plutocracy were becoming bored with her chatter, she nevertheless continued to be received in all the most fashionable circles. She was evidently never dashed by criticism; there were many in Charleston who savored every tidbit of her gossip.

The evening of November 1 was balmy as the celebrated resident strolled past the stately old homes on Meeting Street. It was her wont to amble amidst the oaks, huge magnolias, and white-columned houses as she went back and forth to her usual haunts—her most frequent, the Fort Sumter Hotel on the Battery. On this particular evening, she had not a worry in the world. Cats yowled as she approached Water Street. She was taking in all the evening sights and sounds. The chimes of a church bell suddenly struck the quarter hour. Just at that moment, a man loomed before her. She screamed and raised her right arm to ward off a possible attack. . . . It was over in an instant and her attacker was off. As he ran, he looked back over his shoulder at his victim. Mary screamed a second time and slumped to the ground.

Some minutes later, as Elsa Eberhard drove by the corner of Water and Meeting Streets, she saw what appeared to be a body lying on the sidewalk. Her pulse racing, Elsa drove as fast as she could to a nearby fruit store, where she asked Johnny Townsend, a sophomore at the College of Charleston, for help. He hopped into the car, and they sped to the scene.

Johnny jumped out of the car and turned the body over. "Oh my word," he blurted, "it's Mrs. Ravenel." The thought occurred to Elsa that not only did most of the residents in Charleston know Mary Ravenel, but the students at the college recognized her as well. Mary's purse lay by her side undisturbed, and her expensive jewelry was intact. Suddenly Mrs. Ravenel began to moan and babble incoherently. The two could see that she was injured. They quickly got her into the car and took her to Roper Hospital.

Mary was still conscious when they arrived and was able to give the nurse the name of her physician when asked. The nurse left to place a call to the doctor's home.

"What happened to you?" an attendant asked the patient as they awaited the arrival of the physician.

"A man hit me," Mary responded weakly.

"Was he driving an automobile?" There was no visible wound or bleeding, and since she was able to speak, the hospital staff guessed she had been struck by a car.

"I don't know," she feebly answered.

The nurse returned to say that the physician could not be located and asked Mrs. Ravenel if she had another in mind. Since the patient didn't appear to be severely injured, hospital workers took their time to see that she was treated by a doctor of her choice. She offered the names of two others. Before they arrived, however, Mary Ravenel was dead.

A hospital doctor quickly examined the body and concluded that

Mrs. Ravenel had been stabbed. Before a thorough examination could be made, a car from the funeral home arrived, and the body was taken away to be prepared for burial. Within a few minutes of arrival at the mortician's establishment, a wound was discovered in Mrs. Ravenel's arm. She had been shot.

Dr. Kenneth Lynch, professor of pathology at the Medical College of South Carolina, was summoned to perform an autopsy. During the inspection of the body to determine the cause of death, it was found that the bullet went cleanly through the forearm and pierced Mrs. Ravenel's heart. The bullet was a .38-caliber, copper-jacketed—a type that was not common. There was evidence that it had been hand-filled. No powder burns were found, and it could not be determined from what distance the shot was fired. There was almost no external bleeding; Mrs. Ravenel had died of internal hemorrhaging. The body was bruised, and it was surmised that she had dragged her body a few feet before collapsing.

By this time police had arrived at the scene of the crime. A crowd had gathered, and residents in the area were questioned. Someone had heard a gunshot at a quarter to ten. Another person had heard a cat crying loudly. Someone else had heard a woman scream and a car drive away. Others had heard the steps of a man or woman running. Someone said that Mrs. Ravenel had screamed twice. As the officers summed up the evidence, they found they had little to go on. There was no weapon at the scene and there were no eyewitnesses.

At eleven o'clock on November 3, 1933, as funeral services for Mary Ravenel were being held at her home at 12 Tradd Street, police were no closer to discovering what had happened.

The days passed, and as the authorities continued their investigation, more than forty theories were formulated. Some people believed that the killer was shooting at cats and accidentally hit the woman. But, if that were true, why didn't that person step forward and admit the shooting was an accident? Others believed robbery was the motive, stating that this scenario was supported by the testimony of neighbors who claimed they heard a scream both before and after the pistol shot. The first scream, they said, would indicate that something frightened Mrs. Ravenel. After all, she wouldn't have screamed *before* the shot if she had been hit by a stray bullet meant for a cat. But, if it were robbery, why weren't her jewelry and money taken? Most of those who voiced an opinion did not think Mrs. Ravenel was killed deliberately. She was a pillar in the community, and it was unthinkable to them that she would be gunned down on purpose.

If the death was intentional, it seemed to have been a perfect crime. No one saw it. No gun was found. No motive could be ascertained. The wound was so clean, it wasn't even discovered until after the victim's death.

Still, the investigation continued. On November 27, Robert Cox, a nineteen-year-old Charleston man, was questioned. He lived at 42 Vanderhorst Street, which was not in the immediate vicinity of the crime, but he had already confessed to participation in two store holdups nearby. Cox staunchly denied any connection with the killing of Mrs. Ravenel. No evidence to the contrary was ever found and Cox was not charged.

Mayor Burnet Maybank, in an effort to urge anyone who had a clue to come forward, offered a reward of $250 for "information leading to the apprehension and conviction of the person or persons responsible for the death. . . . no strings attached." The reward went unclaimed.

Three years passed, and during that time many pistols were examined. Not one, however, was the murder weapon. The use of ballistics in identifying guns by the marks made on bullets fired from them was not commonly practiced in Charleston at that time. It was known though that the .38-caliber pistol used in the killing of Mary Ravenel had fired a copper-jacketed, hand-filled bullet.

The Ravenel case was the only unsolved murder case in Charleston at that time. On April 2, 1938, police thought they finally had a lead. William Allen was found dead in Blackstone, Virginia, with a shotgun at his side. In a suicide note found on the body, he confessed to the murder of a local woman and stated that he also had killed a woman in Charleston, South Carolina.

The Ravenel case was immediately reopened. The chief of police detectives left Charleston for Blackstone accompanied by Det. James Atteberry. After a full investigation, the officers concluded that Allen was not the murderer of Mrs. Ravenel. Furthermore, they believed that he had called attention to Charleston only because a divorced wife lived there at the time the note was written. The detectives believed the mention of Charleston to be for the purpose of embarrassing his former wife. Wise and Atteberry returned home and the case was again put to rest.

Just when it seemed the perfect crime really had been committed, nature took a hand in the unraveling of events—at least that's what some people believe.

It was September 28, 1938. All was calm on the peninsula of magnificent and historic homes. As the people of Charleston lay snug in their high-poster beds on that Wednesday night, they were unaware that a small tropical disturbance had formed in the Gulf of Mexico and was moving east.

By Thursday morning, low-hanging clouds, pushed by strong upper winds, covered the city. One James Island woman stood on the widow's walk of her house, surveying the sky as her children got ready for school and her husband drove into the city. The sight her eyes beheld was ominous. A huge, black funnel cloud, which only minutes before had touched down at Edisto Island, twisting huge trees and exploding houses, was now dropping onto James Island. The woman rushed downstairs to gather her children into the middle of the house.

At about eight o'clock, several men standing outside a gas station saw the black spout approaching from the west bank of the Ashley River. It sucked up water as it crossed the river and continued to increase in velocity. As the tornado reached the river bridge, it lifted a huge truck, spun it around, and dumped the shattered wreck on the ground. The men were horrified as they watched the massive cloud approach. In an instant the roof of the gas station flew off and splintered.

Robert Aldridge, the meterologist at the local weather bureau, was making a call about the storm when he spotted a second funnel, following almost precisely the same path as the first. "My God, a second one is coming!" he shouted.

City Hall trembled, the high steeple of St. Philips Church swayed, and winds that sounded like a hundred locomotives smashed onto Meeting Street, King Street, Water Street, and South Battery. The mighty twister snaked its way to East Bay and Market Streets. The walls of the Charleston Paper Company building bulged outward and the roof collapsed. Masonry columns supporting the heavy slate roof of the old market gave way, crushing more than a dozen people. Docks at the Charleston Shipbuilding and Drydock Company were destroyed.

A lesser storm had now crashed onto the peninsula and damaged the Carolina Yacht Club and Clyde Line terminal. North of the city, two more tornadoes were touching down here and there, teasing frightened people who were crouching under furniture in hope of saving their lives.

By half past eight, all was quiet. Then came the sirens, as every available nurse and physician tended the injured. Marines and sailors from the Charleston Navy Yard, troops from Fort Moultrie, and marines from Parris Island rushed to the stricken city. Hundreds of Works Progress Administration (WPA) workers came to help. From the air the paths of the tornadoes were tracked. The pilots were astonished at the devastation.

A hole gaped in the roof of St. Michael's Church. The fourth floor of a hotel had disappeared. The old Confederate Home on Broad Street had been severely hurt. Mrs. Ravenel's old haunt, the Fort Sumter Hotel, was damaged. Not a window remained in the city hall building. Automobiles were overturned and some had been tossed through store windows. Hundreds of people were injured, and thirty-two were dead.

"The Day of the Tornadoes," as that day is now called, yielded an unexpected surprise. As the city, aided by funds from the federal government, began to rebuild, a crew was sent to a shattered house on Price's Alley. It was the home of Payne, the photographer Mrs. Ravenel so blatantly gossiped about. As they searched the basement, they saw that a filing cabinet had fallen over during the storm. Under the filing cabinet lay a gun. When a bullet was found in the chamber, Det. Herman Berkman was called to take a look.

"It's a .38-caliber, all right," the officer remarked. "And the copper-jacketed bullet has been hand-filled. It's a dead ringer for the bullet found in Mrs. Ravenel."

The gun was sent to the F.B.I. for tests, but it was so badly damaged by salt water, no positive identification could be made. Regardless of what the tests failed to prove, Detective Berkman was convinced that Payne had murdered Mrs. Ravenel. With no evidence, however, and the more pressing matter of storm cleanup to handle, the Ravenel case was left officially unsolved.

What do you, the reader, think? In spite of the lack of *official* evidence, was the mystery behind the death of Mary Ravenel really solved that day?

Rebellion

Capt. John Vesey commanded a ship that traded in slaves for the San Domingo French. The ship plied between St. Thomas and Cape Francis, San Domingo. On a routine trip in 1781 Captain Vesey took onboard at St. Thomas 390 slaves and set sail for Cape Francis.

Vesey and his officers were impressed by a boy of fourteen, because of his "beauty, alertness and intelligence." They made a sort of pet of him and named him Telemaque, a name that later was corrupted to Telmark and then to Denmark.

Denmark was indeed fortunate to have been taken aboard Vesey's ship.

John Vesey was born in 1747 in Warwick, Bermuda. He spent much of his life on the seas. On March 1, 1775, he was commissioned to haul fifteen tons of Madeira wine to Charles Town on the *Rebecca*. He made his delivery and immediately departed for Madeira for a second load. This work brought Vesey to the old port city for the first time.

Later, for the South Carolina Navy, Vesey commanded the *Hawke* and sailed to Philadelphia to secure recruits. During the Revolutionary War he served on the brig *Hornet* and as lieutenant on the sloop *Providence* under John Paul Jones.

Capt. John Vesey was a man of principle who endeavored to do his job in as humane a way as possible. He was knowledgeable about the ways of the world.

Denmark was treated kindly on Vesey's ship and received more freedom than other slaves onboard. He was, nevertheless, put ashore at Cape Francis, where he was to serve one of the French planters at St. Dominigue.

Denmark was returned to Captain Vesey after only three months because of his alleged unsoundness. It was also asserted that he was subject to epileptic seizures. Vesey was required to take him back. Denmark became the captain's personal servant and had plenty of opportunity during his time at sea to increase his skill with languages. In addition to English, he heard French and Spanish spoken onboard. Vesey saw to it that the youth was provided with an extensive cosmopolitan education, and he gave him his own name.

During the next twenty years Denmark claimed to be faithful to Vesey. In 1800 he unexpectedly won $1,500 in Charleston's East Bay Street Lottery, and he purchased his freedom for $600. After that time he earned his living by trade, as a carpenter and joiner. Having been employed on shipboard, traveled a great deal of the world, and acquired a wealth of knowledge, Denmark Vesey was regarded as a leading man among the Charleston black population. He enjoyed a kind of liberty that would have satisfied most persons of his status, and he owned property valued at $8,000. At the age of fifty-five some might have believed him to be beyond the age of ambition, but that was not the case with Denmark Vesey.

About that time Vesey became concerned with the condition of human bondage that existed in South Carolina. In Charleston, free women of color were not allowed to wear veils about their faces in the streets, or in any public place. A violation of that law was visited with thirty-nine lashes upon the bare back. The same was inflicted upon any free man of color who was seen upon the streets with a cigar in his mouth or a walking stick in his hand. While such odious edicts were silently borne in 1822 by the slaves of Charleston and the surrounding countryside, there was a suppressed feeling of indignation, mortification, and discontent appreciated by more than a few of the freed men. The most dissatisfied of that group was Denmark Vesey. He began embittering the minds of slaves against their white masters. If, while walking through the streets with a slave, that slave bowed to a white man, Vesey would rebuke him. If the slave said, "I am a slave," Vesey would retort, "And you deserve to remain a slave." Vesey was a religious man, and he sought justification for his action in the Bible. He believed the Bible showed that God wanted slaves to be free, and he used scripture to indoctrinate his followers. His favorite texts were Joshua 6:21,

Zachariah 14:1–3, and Luke 11:23. In all his conversations, Vesey compared the slaves' situation with that of the Israelites.

Vesey made substantial progress in winning support from the more learned slaves, particularly from leaders of the African Church who were already nursing grievances against Charleston's white authority because of the suppression of their work. As he continued his underground campaign, Vesey's temper became impetuous and domineering. His passions were sometimes ungovernable and savage, and one day while in that black mood he worked out a plan for a slave uprising in the city. Denmark Vesey's plan was patterned after those of two of his heroes: Henry Christophe and Touissant L'Ouverture, leaders in the bloody insurrection of 1793 that resulted in the killing of all whites who failed to escape from the island of Hispaniola (Haiti-Santo Domingo). Vesey's plan was carefully laid out at meetings in his home and in the African Church.

Vesey selected Peter Poyas, a slave of superior foresight and ability, as his lieutenant. Poyas was said to have an "evil eye." When he set his gaze on a person, that person was rendered unable to resist anything Poyas dictated. Poyas appointed three men as generals in the brigade: Gullah Jack, a root doctor and healer; Ned Bennett; and Tom Russell. Secrets of the uprising were surrendered only to these men. Russell was ingenuous as a mechanic, and he made battle axes, pikes, and other instruments of death.

Vesey continued his work of embittering the minds of slaves against their masters, without disclosing his intentions. His work was taking effect. Sunday, July 14, 1822, was the date chosen for the uprising. Country slaves were permitted to visit the city in great numbers on Sunday, but had to return home in time to commence their tasks on the following morning. A prayer meeting was scheduled for the Sunday on which the uprising would take place. The battle plan would be announced at that meeting. Angolas, Eboes, and Carolina-born slaves were organized, and special plans were laid for all of them, including the slaves on the surrounding plantations. Vesey told his chosen few that a haven would be provided aboard vessels in Charleston's harbor in the event the uprising should be sufficiently successful to permit seizure of ships.

The plan dictated that on the Sunday of the massacre, Peter Poyas was to lead a party to South Bay. This group was to be joined by a force from James Island. The assembled company was to seize the arsenal and Guard House opposite St. Michael's Church.

Permanent regimental orders at the Guard Houses of Charleston were as follows:

> In case of alarm from fire, the bells only will ring, and then the Fire Guard only will parade. In case of a serious alarm, the drums will beat to Arms, and the Cannon will be fired at the Guard House. On such alarm the place of rendezvous is at the corner of State and Queen streets. To this place you must instantly hasten, properly armed and accoutered. Our families must be left for a moment to ensure them protection, which will be promptly afforded by Guards selected for that purpose. Disgrace will forever attend every man who shall not on such an alarm instantly force his way to his Company Muster Ground.

A second company, composed of slaves from the country and the "Neck," the inland portion of the peninsula that formed Charleston, was to be led by Ned Bennett. They were to assemble on the Neck and seize the arsenal there. A third company was to put the governor to death and march through the city. A fourth was to gather at Gadsden's Wharf and attack the upper Guard House.

A fifth company was to gather at Denmark Vesey's house and follow his orders, while Gullah Jack was to assemble his men in Boundary Street and secure arms from Mr. Duquerreroa's shop. Naval stores in Mey's Wharf were to be attacked.

A total of nine thousand slaves would be involved. Once the city was taken, a mounted force would patrol the streets. Every white man who attempted to leave his house would be killed.

On May 30, 1822, George, bodyguard of Mr. Wilson, reported to his master that Mr. Paul's slave William had invited him to join in an attempt for freedom to be won by the massacre of white masters. William was seized by the city council and questioned. He alleged that Mingo Harth and Peter Poyas had enlisted him in the plot. Harth and Poyas were picked up and questioned. Both denied the allegation and were discharged, but they were kept under constant observation. William, imprisoned for a week, disclosed the plot and the date that was set for the uprising. Upon this news, the city guard was strengthened and the local militia called to be ready for action.

Duvany, a slave belonging to Colonel Prioleau, heard of the planned uprising and went to his master with the information. Prioleau went at once to the mayor and informed him of the plan of insurrection. The city council was called together for a consultation. Slaves throughout the city were questioned, but all claimed ignorance of any plan. The authorities had begun to feel that they had been involved in trickery, when another conspirator revealed what he knew.

On Monday, June 17, as arrests were being made, Denmark Vesey went into hiding. Not until June 22 was he found, during a violent storm, hold up in the home of one of his wives. He would probably have effected his escape the following day by boarding a sea vessel if the city guard had not seized him that evening.

A trial was held on Wednesday, June 19, three days before the capture of Vesey, presided over by two magistrates and five freeholders. It was a legitimate court, its jurists were eminently qualified judges, and its procedures followed the state's code of law.

On June 25, 1822, the dissolution of the most elaborate insurrection project ever formed by American slaves began. Of the 131 arrested, 38 were released for lack of evidence and 93 went to trial. Of those tried, 67 were convicted, and 26 acquitted. Of the individuals convicted, 35 were hanged and 42 banished from the state. Denmark Vesey was found quilty and executed.

The incident left slaveholders in fear. Plantations began to be patrolled by men called "patrollers," and guards were doubled in the city. A great crisis had, for the present, been averted.

A more complicated plan for an insurrection could scarcely have been conceived than that devised by Denmark Vesey. The Denmark Vesey conspiracy was the beginning of a number of slave revolts that continued almost until the end of the Civil War.

Lost at Sea

Miles Brewton was born January 29, 1731. Although he may be rememberd by historians as a man who gave service to his country—elected to the first Provincial Congress June 1775 and the second Provincial Congress August 1775—he is remembered by old Charlestonians and visitors to the port city as the man who built the elegant colonial residence at No. 27 King Street. Construction on the house was begun shortly after Brewton's marriage to Mary Izard on May 19, 1759.

Brewton, a wealthy Charleston businessman and leader, chose as his builder Ezra Waite of London, civil architect, house builder, and carver. The "high Georgian" style and masterful workmanship qualify the Miles Brewton House as one of the finest architectural triumphs of the late eighteenth century.

Built on a large lot, extending from King Street to Legare, the house was constructed of brick and stone brought from England. An English landscape architect designed the back garden, which was divided by wide walks covered in seashells from the West Indies. Rows of orange trees lined the walks and pear trees stood among the shrubbery.

The house faces King Street and one enters through heavy iron gates and chevaux-de-frises. Stone steps lead up to a stone portico where heavy white columns of Portland stone painted white support the roof. All wood and stone features on the portico are richly carved, testifying to Waite's mastery as a carver. Inside, doors along the broad hallway open to the left and right. At the end of the hall a handsome stairway leads up to the drawing room on the second floor. That drawing room, beautifully proportioned, features a high arched ceiling and an exquisite Waterford chandelier. Among the portraits on the walls is one of Miles Brewton in pink silk doublet, painted in London in 1756 by Joshua Reynolds.

Brewton's great-grandson J. Motte Alston wrote that as one entered the house, the room on the left was called the yellow parlor, for the color of the damask upholstered furniture and draperies. He spoke of large mirrors on the walls, a beautiful marble mantel, and white doves in fresco on the ceiling.

The reported cost of the house was eight thousand pounds sterling.

The attic was stocked with pipes of Madeira, as well as port, Lisbon, and Sauterne wine. There was also ale and demijohns of French brandy, rum, and Irish whiskey. Many heads of household in Charles Town consumed two bottles of Madeira daily. One such man was John Rutledge, whose home on Broad Street was not far from the Brewton mansion.

Miles Brewton was the perfect host, and famous people, such as Josiah Quincy, Jr., and Lord William Campbell, were among those he entertained.

When the Brewton house was still practically new, there was much talk about war with England. The possibility of a battle at Sullivans Island, across the bay from Charleston, worried many of the women. Mary Brewton was the nervous type, and she fretted over such an eventuality. During the very time she was luxuriating in the talk of the top quality workmanship of her new home, she was begging her husband to take her and their children north until the trouble blew over. Miles Brewton owned half interest in a seafaring vessel, and he made plans to set sail for Philadelphia.

Looking back at Charles Town as they sailed away from the city, they must have bid a sad farewell to their magnificent mansion and thought with great sadness of the valuable possessions being left behind.

As they traveled toward Philadelphia, Mary Brewton was edgy and insisted the vessel's captain sail close to shore and drop anchor every night. The captain objected, saying that dropping anchor each night would double the time of the voyage, and he needed to move ahead quickly due to approaching bad weather. Mary stood firm, and the vessel never ventured far from the seashore.

One night the sea was uncommonly rough and its roaring frightened those on shipboard as well as those living along the coast. The next morning the storm moderated, but by evening it had returned and doubled in force. On shore, trees were uprooted. The wind continued to increase in violence, driving ocean spray for miles inland. Vessels along the shore were blown away and others washed to sea. The amount of property destroyed was incalculable, and all wharves along that stretch of coast and on nearby rivers were washed away. No one ever heard from the Brewton vessel again.

The will of Miles Brewton, having been made on July 16, 1778, mentioned his wife Mary and their sons, and other family members. His large estate, which included many sets of porcelain china, crystal, silver, paintings, oriental rugs, and his beautiful home on King Street, as well as a plantation, were divided between his two sisters. Frances Brewton Pinckney and Rebecca Brewton Motte. His sister Rebecca came to live in the Charles Town mansion. As she viewed the furnishings of the mansion, she discovered in an armoire a quiver of East Indian arrows, which, when fired, would burst into flame after hitting their targets. The arrows had been brought from the East Indies by a sea captain and presented to Miles Brewton as a gift. The case that held the arrows was a long dark brown bamboo quiver, with figures carved in a lighter shade of brown. Rebecca Motte used the quiver as a knitting needle case.

Mrs. Motte also took possession of her brother's plantation on the Congaree River, in the Orangeburg District. She was living there in 1781 with her three daughters and Mrs. John Brewton when the British took possession of the house for a military post. Mrs. Motte and her family were permitted to remain in the house for a time, but the British soldiers eventually suggested she move into her overseer's house. To this, she fiercely objected.

On May 8, 1781, Gen. Francis Marion appeared on the plantation. There was a meeting of military strategy, and Mrs. Motte was gingerly informed that the house might have to be destroyed to be rid of the British. She immediately and cheerfully consented, assuring the Patriots that the loss of her property was nothing compared to the advancement of the cause. To facilitate the operations, she presented General Marion with the combustible arrows. The arrows were discharged from a rifle. The first two did not ignite, but the third set the roof on fire. The British surrendered the house immediately, and the fire was extinguished. The house was saved.

The Daughters Were in the Attic

Rebecca Brewton, sister of Miles Brewton who built the beautiful mansion at 27 King Street in Charles Town, was born on June 15, 1737. On June 28, 1758, she married Jacob Motte, son of Jacob Motte, Public Treasurer of South Carolina. Rebecca and Jacob had seven children. Three daughters, Elizabeth, Frances, and Mary, survived to live with their mother at the Miles Brewton house.

Rebecca Motte and her daughters were living in the Miles Brewton House in 1780, when the city was seized by Lord Rawdon and Col. Nesbit Balfour, Commandant of Charleston. Sir Henry Clinton exhibited exceptional taste, for he could not have chosen a more beautiful place to use as headquarters when Charleston surrendered to the British on May 12 than the Miles Brewton House.

Constructed of brick in 1765 upon a high basement with arched divisions of solid masonry, the house has two stories and features a pitched tiled roof.

The house was entered from the portico through a large door with a fanlight above it. The door, which was set in a handsome carved frame, opened into a wide flagged hall with two large rooms on each side. The drawing rooms made up the entire east front. The walls of all reception and dining rooms were paneled and featured heavy cornices. Mantels were fashioned of marble in the high narrow style of the day. Doors throughout the house were of polished mahogany, as were the balusters and fittings of the stairs. The attic was used as storage for wines and furniture.

Although the advance on Charleston by sea in 1780 did not take place until July 1, the city surrendered to the British on May 12. By that time, Gov. John Rutledge had fled Charleston for Georgetown.

When the British military leaders announced they were taking over the Miles Brewton House for use as headquarters, they requested that Rebecca Motte remain and act as their hostess, presiding over meals. She accepted their invitation with cold disdain. While the British officers talked over their good fortune, Mrs. Motte hurriedly stampeded her three beautiful daughters up into the attic. She explained to them that she was keeping them a secret from the Englishmen, and they must make little or no noise in order to keep their whereabouts a secret.

Old posts and beams supported the peaked roof in the attic, a quirky space that Mrs. Motte turned into the children's bedroom. The daughters did not object, as they had occasionally used the attic as a playroom. The beds stored there were stacked with several feather mattresses, making it necessary to use steps to climb up onto them, and the girls had especially enjoyed playing on these. The attic windows looked out onto Charleston church spires, chimneys, and gabled roofs.

During the time that Mrs. Motte sat as hostess of the long dining room table, she occasionally excused herself to go to the attic for wine. Of course, she slipped trays of food to her daughters. As the officers consumed much Madeira, Mrs. Motte made frequent attic visits, using the excuse that she could make an excellent choice of wine from the large inventory she had on hand. She constantly reminded her daughters that she was harboring the enemy, and they must not let anyone know they were in the house. The camouflage seemed to be working, but the daughters were getting on one another's nerves. They were enduring endless hours of boredom, and when they slept, they repeatedly woke up afraid, their slumber having been shattered by bolts of stupefying terror.

During his stay in the house one of the British officers carved a profile of the head of commanding officer Sir Henry Clinton on one of the marble mantels. He carved Clinton's swords above the image of his head and etched the outline of a full-rigged ship. Some say he used the point of a bayonet; others believe his tool was a diamond ring.

Other damage was done to the house during its occupation. An

Englishman thrust a sword into the valued portrait of Miles Brewton, painted in London by Joshua Reynolds in 1756. Mrs. Motte's heart must have leapt as she witnessed the desecration of her home. Could she have recognized, despite her pain, the historical value of those mementos of the English occupation that would mark the house forever?

Before leaving Charles Town for New York on June 3, Sir Henry Clinton took Mrs. Motte's hands in his as he bid her farewell. He thanked her for all her kindnesses, the superb meals so elegantly served, and the fine Madeira wine so frequently brought down from the attic. Having said that, he rolled his eyes upward and said his only regret was in not meeting the rest of her family.

NOTE: The Miles Brewton House descended through five generations of women family members. During the time it was in the possession of three sisters, Mary Pringle Frost, Susan P. Frost, and Rebecca Motte Frost, the house was opened for public viewing. Miss Mary Pringle Frost wrote a little booklet called *Meaning of a House*, in which she said

> My Sister [Susan Frost] and I . . . feel that this house should be known and loved by the community and . . . it should live side by side with smaller houses in its love for what is true and friendly.
> A house needs friends: it needs interchange of human thought: it is a human habitation. What would a habitation be without an inhabitant? It would be lonely; its spirit would faint.

> *O floors that felt our life-long tread,*
> *Windows whence babes peeped at their stars,*
> *Thresholds whence passed away our dead,*
> *O'er which our brides came from afar!*

For those who go into the attic of the home at 27 King Street, it must be hard *not* to feel the presence of the three daughters there.

The Murder Trial
of Stephen Denaro

On Tuesday, December 2, 1879, brothers Moses and John Denaro visited the office of the coroner of Charleston County. They gave affidavits that on the fifteenth of the previous September their father, Stephen Denaro, who kept a store on Edisto Island, killed "Singing Jack" Williams. Asked why they had not previously told of the slaying, they replied that they had not done so because of threats made to them by their father. The coroner remembered Stephen Denaro. He had been in trouble seven years earlier for having tried to poison a man.

A deputy sheriff was contacted by the coroner. The deputy went to Edisto where he arrested the elder Denaro without incident. On the drive to Charleston, Denaro was informed of the charge against him. He denied any knowledge of the crime and claimed his sons had fabricated the story because they desired his property.

The case came to trial in the Court of General Sessions in Charleston during February 1880. Because of more than usual interest in the case, the courtroom was crowded with spectators. In addition to many curious Charlestonians, the courthouse staff slipped into the courtroom for a look at the defendant. They were disappointed when he entered. Instead of the powerful physique they expected, they saw a small, wiry, sallow-faced man of about fifty years, with black hair, a small black mustache, and small dark eyes.

There were connected with the trial of this case some leading Charleston attorneys. The defendant was represented by Maj. Theodore G. Parker and James P. Lesesne, while solicitor W. St. Julien Jervey acted for the state.

The two sons, who lived on Fig Island about five miles from Edisto where they worked for Singing Jack as caretakers of his livestock, were in the courtroom as witnesses for the state. They testified that on September 15, 1879, their father Stephen Denaro arrived at their place about midnight and urged them and Williams to go raccoon hunting with him. Setting out on the hunt, the senior Denaro led the way, walking ahead with Singing Jack; the two boys followed. The group had not gone far when an argument began between the two in front. Stephen Denaro suddenly attacked Williams with a hatchet, inflicting several severe cuts and causing instant death. Denaro then demanded that his sons help dig a grave. The slain man was buried in a shallow hole near the spot where he fell.

In his testimony, Moses claimed that his father had committed four previous murders—one in 1873, one in 1875, and two in 1876. The murders were not proven. The defendant, in his testimony, charged that the two boys had accused him so they could get his money and keep it from their stepmother, whom they disliked. A Charleston attorney testified that shortly after the arrest of the father, the sons had solicited his aid in securing the father's money. He informed them that as their father was not yet dead, he could dispose of his property as he saw fit. The boys had responded with "He's as good as dead already."

Defense attorneys endeavored to impeach the testimony of the sons, claiming they had accused the father of the four murders in the hope of reward and that subsequently they had charged him with the Williams murder. The case finally went to the jury.

After a deliberation of several hours, the jury could not agree and the case was declared a mistrial. The case came up for trial again during the June term of that year. At that time the accused was acquitted, thus ending one of the most memorable murder trials in Charleston history.

The trial was obviously not enough to keep Stephen Denaro out of trouble. He was indicted in 1883 on a charge of carrying concealed weapons. The charge, however, was discontinued and never brought to trial.

The House Built for Love

Irish immigrant Patrick O'Donnell built the mansion at 21 King Street for the woman he loved, and he intended it to be her home.

No expense was spared in construction and the resulting home was one of the most beautiful in Charleston. The house was much stronger structurally than was usual in buildings constructed in the mid-1800s. This was evident in the size of the boards and beams, the thickness of the brickwork, and many other of its structural details.

The architecture was typically Charleston, with long, columned piazzas extending back from the street. Italianate in style, the traditional single-house plan was modified by the addition of a slightly recessed window on the north side containing the formal entrance hall and stairs. Each tier of the piazza had a different entablature atop each of its fluted Doric columns. The architect, Edward C. Jones of Charleston, effectively accomplished the exterior look of an eighteenth-century Venetian palazzo, while the interior had the feel of a New York brownstone townhouse. The entry door was massive, standing above a flight of steep brownstone steps that were crafted to match the scale of the building.

Seashells and other sea creatures were carved into the woodwork around the second-floor windows. The face of Jenny Lind, "the Swedish Nightingale," appeared repeatedly in the ceiling medallions in the double drawing rooms. Cast iron gas lamps were installed to provide light.

The construction of the mansion consumed the majority of Patrick O'Connell's time and by the date of completion the intended bride had fallen in love with someone else and eloped.

O'Donnell was half crazy with grief. During the nights that followed, he wandered the mansion considering his fate. The main house, the library section, the kitchen wing—all so beautiful. Outside, his eyes followed the Italian Renaissance styling, soaring skyward. He noted the well-balanced proportions of the building that offset the heavy decorations on the facade. All for nothing! The Galway Irishman had many beautiful bedrooms, but no wife to help fill them.

O'Donnell never overcame his grief. He lived as a recluse and remained a bachelor until his death in 1882. His last will and testament stipulated his estate be administered by a priest, Father Tom Burke of the Order of St. Dominick. O'Donnell's property was to be used for the good of the poor of his native Galway.

Even in death, O'Donnell's house was not used according to his wishes, as his executor made off with most of the money. The Bishop of Galway sued the executor, but the money had been spent. O'Donnell owned other Charleston properties, but all in all, it profited the poor of Galway only about $12,000.

The house at 21 King Street, which had become known as "O'Donnell's Folly," was purchased by Thomas Riley McGahan, another Gael and a Charleston merchant, who became a blockade runner during the Civil War. McGahan's wife, Emma Fourgeaud, whose ancestors had barely escaped the bloody massacres by slaves in the Santo Domingan revolution, was a cousin of Margaret Mitchell. Mitchell was so impressed with the romantic idea of the escape of the Fourgeauds that she modeled her *Gone with the Wind* character Melanie Wilkes after Emma.

The next owner of O'Donnell's Folly was Thomas Pinckney whose daughter, Josephine, was just reaching her teens.

Mr. and Mrs. Frederick Rutledge Baker bought the house before World War II, and it has had other owners through the years.

Although a number of women have loved and called this beautiful place *home*, the woman for whom the romantic house was built never lived there. Knowing this, some people experience a sort of sadness when they view the magnificent structure.

Charleston's Secret
Millionaires Club

Once upon a time there was a club for millionaires near Charleston. The club manager, Tom Pochman, told the *Evening Post*, "The club prefers no publicity at all." He declined to discuss the matter further. Although huge white yachts rode at anchor in the harbor and private railroad cars stood on sidings, neighbors of Yeamans Hall Club in Goose Creek did not know the club existed. Today there are few people who can offer information about the days when Clare Boothe Luce hunted and dined with the likes of Hugh D. Auchincloss, stepfather of Jacqueline Kennedy Onassis, and other club members whose names represented many of the wealthiest families in the country. The members were content to pay huge club fees for the privileges of Yeamans Hall, using the club only a few weeks during each year. The club opened officially December 15, but there was usually a large group of the two hundred members on hand at Thanksgiving, when the club served the customary "Old Thanksgiving" dinner.

Thirty-seven "cottages" surrounded the main building, a sprawling and hospitable structure with a country club aura located on land for which Lady Margaret Yeamans received title for herself and many servants. The grant was made "9 Febr'y 1674/5 for 1070 acres bounding upon Yeamans Creeke in Ittawan River."

Sir John Yeamans, husband of Lady Margaret, on January 11, 1665, received a commission as lieutenant general and governor of Carolina. The Lords Proprietors had received a good report of his abilities and loyalty and they had induced the king to confer the honor of a Knight Baronet upon him and his heirs. Under this commission, Sir John Yeamans organized an expedition to set out from Barbados for Carolina to explore its lower coast and select a proper site for settlement. These "adventurers," as they were called, believed that settlers could produce in Carolina "wines, currents, raisins, silks, etc., the planting of which will not injure other plantations, which may very well happen if there were a great increase of sugar works or more tobacco, ginger, cotton, and indigo made than the world will vent." Sir John died in July or August 1674, prior to the date of the grant of property to his wife. It is altogether improbable that Sir John Yeamans ever resided upon the property.

In 1695 the property was sold to Landgrave Thomas Smith, one of the leaders in the early Charles Town colony and, later, governor. Smith and his wife built a house and named it "Goose Creek Mansion." The house, constructed of brick said to have been brought over from England, was a two-story structure, almost square, with a basement beneath and a broad verandah in front. The interior was described by an early chronicler as elegantly finished. Anna Cornelia Smith carried with her to the Goose Creek mansion the portrait of her relative, the beautiful Sabina de Vignon, Landgrave Thomas Smith's second wife. [This portrait hung on the mansion's wall until the Revolution, when a British officer cut it out of its frame and took the lovely Sabina with him.] The walls were painted in panels representing landscapes and hung with tapestries. Large fireplaces were lined with blue and white Dutch tiles that depicted Biblical scenes. Handsome cornices and moldings decorated the rooms.

Entering from the front, one came into a large hall, with an immense chimney. Doors led off this hall to other rooms. One door gave access to the rear of the house, from which a staircase led to the upper story. A secret chamber in a closet at the back of the structure provided access between the walls of the upper and lower stories through a concealed trap door.

The house remained in the Smith family for two hundred years, occasionally suffering neglect. In 1850, Eliza F. Smith, who owned the house at that time, changed the name from "Goose Creek Mansion" to "Yeamans Hall," remembering that the land had originally belonged to the Yeamans family. Yeamans Hall was badly shaken by the earthquake of August 1886, and two years later it was almost destroyed by fire, leaving only a few of the exterior walls standing.

The first interest in establishing a resort for *quiet* northern millionaires at this site came in 1915 when Edward W. Durant, Jr., vice president of Burton Lumber Company, took the noted architect, Frederick Law Olmstead, on a tour of the property. Burton Lumber Company at that time owned most of the land that is now North Charleston. Henry K. Getchius of New York, wealthy and retired, also became interested in the tract of land. Getchius had planned to invest in Florida real estate, but then saw the Yeamans Hall property. The ruins of the old mansion, the beautiful live oaks, and the rolling lands, situated only about twenty miles from Charleston, captivated him. He realized it was a perfect location for some sort of sportsmen's club—the hunting in that particular area was of the best. Getchius also saw the potential for a golf course.

In 1924 Yeamans Hall Company purchased a nine-hundred-acre tract from a Charleston consortium headed by R. Goodwyn Rhett. Work on the first golf course, planned by Donald Ross, began in 1924. Complete plans for Yeamans Hall Club called for about 150 buildings, including a clubhouse, club cottages, and private homes that would be reached by winding roads. The layout, architecture, and landscape would combine modern and colonial styles. The property included not only some of the most beautiful and valuable timber and woodlands in the South Carolina Low Country, but three springs: the Silver Cup, the Gold Cup, and the Governor's Springs. The club represented a total investment of $2 million and an annual upkeep expense of about $175,000.

Seventeen houses were ready for the 1929/30 season. Grantland Rice (1880–1954), U. S. journalist who viewed the golf course on his way to Florida, called it "the most beautiful in the country." Members of the board of governors included Sterling W. Childs of New York, president; John Peyton Clark of Charleston, vice president; Leonard D. Baldwin of New York, secretary and treasurer; Alfred M. Coats of Providence, Rhode Island; Julius Day of New Haven, Connecticut; R. Goodwyn Rhett and E. W. Durant of Charleston; Louis Hey of New York; and Edward H. Floyd Jones of Massapequa, Long Island, New York. New members included the chairman of the board of Chase National Bank of New York and a former assistant United States attorney general, as well as others who were tantamount to a "Who's Who" of achievement in America. The membership of two hundred was reached. The names of others who desired to become members were put on a waiting list.

Several piers were constructed on Goose Creek, a tributary of the Cooper River—one pier for the general use of members, other piers private. M. M. Gardner, president of the Massachusetts Golf Association, believed that the golf course was perfect, saying "When you leave you cannot think of a single weak hole."

By 1931 Yeamans Hall had taken its place as one of the most notable developments of its kind in the South. It was a winter colony whose membership was confined largely to wealthy men of the North, a large number of whom were members of the board of governors of the New York Stock Exchange. The membership included Seth L. Pierrepont of Ridgefield, Connecticut; Nicholas G. Roosevelt of Philadelphia; Hugh D. Auchincloss of New York; Edward S. Harkness of New York; Alfred Huger of Charleston; Scott McLanahan of New York; Mrs. Henry Van Cleef of New Haven; and Mrs. Howard F. Whitney of New York, among other notables. The organization of the club brought about the establishment of a new aristocracy in the South Carolina Low Country—individuals moneyed and with a taste for the things the old planters loved. The newcomers occupied and restored the lands the descendants of the rice planters saw crumbling, losing their former glory.

About $2 million had been invested in Yeamans Hall, and five private homes were being completed. Those homes were scattered throughout the woods surrounding the club. The forests were beautiful and provided the perfect background and asylum for each mansion. The owners developed the surrounding grounds as they saw fit. The magazine *House Beautiful* awarded the home of Charles N. Mason of New York first prize in their fifth annual small house competition for homes built east of the Mississippi. The home was pictured in the magazine, although the Yeamans Hall desired no publicity. The pillared porch was one of the main features of the Mason mansion; it was placed at the rear to insure privacy. Walls were of brick veneer, painted white, and the roof was of rose-colored Georgian clay tile. An interesting point was the arrangement of low wings, with connecting arched loggias, which created an effect of spaciousness and hospitality and provided extra bedrooms on the ground floor. The house fronted on the fairway of the club's golf course. The oval breakfast room featured a dado rail from an old Charleston house and white wall with a border of antique wallpaper. Mason was the owner and president of Electrical Securities Corporation, 1020 Fifth Avenue, New York. He was also director of the Carolina Power and Light Company and of many other public utility corporations, as well as numerous foundations and associations.

Although the members of Yeamans Hall were not warned or notified, on October 3, 1934, federal agents raided Charleston's Carolina Yacht Club, Elks Club, and Hibernian Hall. Moonshine liquor was seized both at the Yacht Club and at the Elks Club. The government's policy was to halt the sale of illegal liquor in the clubs. In 1935, acting alone, Samuel Gershon, an agent of the federal alcohol beverage unit, raided Yeamans Hall. From this incident the club not only received the publicity it did not want, but negative publicity at that.

After searching the bar, which operated on the first floor of the clubhouse, the agent asked to be shown where the liquor was kept. He was taken to the storeroom. Apparently no illegal liquor was being served at the bar, but twelve cases—Scotch, bourbon, and champagne—were found in the storeroom, some owned by the club management, others by individual residents. Tags on the burlap sacks in which the liquor was stored indicated the names of the owners. Gershon declined to divulge the names, but said, "They are prominent."

All the liquor, with the exception of two quarts of South Carolina *corn*, was confiscated. Some of the contraband seized was as old as twenty years. Included was Haig's Gold Label, a rare blend that had been discontinued.

Years later, during World War II, the privacy of Yeamans Hall was again interrupted when some of the cottages were made available as housing to military personnel stationed in the area.

Charleston's persistent newspaper reporters tried every way possible to write a feature story on the club and have photographs taken, but they were unable to break the privacy curtain. That privacy, of course, was one of the main attractions of such a retreat and one which the members cherished and guarded. By 1963, the people of Charleston who had learned of the exclusive millionaire's club protested that they had not even had a peek at the property. For the first time the plantation was opened to the public and a tour was scheduled for a Sunday afternoon during springtime, when the gardens would be at their peak of bloom. The tour, which took place 2:00 to 5:30 PM, was arranged for benefit of Historic Charleston Foundation and its preservation work in Charleston. Visitors meandered through the private grounds of Yeamans Hall Club and eight private homes of club members, all a part of the original plantation. The gardens' owners were Mr. and Mrs. Donald R. Baldwin of New York; Mrs. John Jay Pierrepont of Ridgefield, Connecticut; Dr. and Mrs. David W. Gaiser of Spokane, Washington; Mrs. John P. Wilson of Chicago; Mr. and Mrs. Joseph France of Baltimore; Mr. and Mrs. William C. Riker of Rumson, New Jersey; Mr. and Mrs. Samuel Borom; and Mr. and Mrs. Phillip W. Nash.

The Yeamans Hall Club still exists at the end of Yeamans Road, behind the privacy and exclusivity curtain with which it opened. As in the old days, the community is not open to the public, and it is difficult to get a peek at what lies beyond the gate. It is known, however, that Hurricane Hugo took down many of the old moss-draped oaks when it struck Charleston in September 1989. Some of the original houses have been remodeled. Children who live in homes on the old plantation attend local private schools. The clubhouse is still there. The railroad, where private railroad cars once stood, is still there. Goose Creek, where private yachts rode at anchor still flows. Yeamans Hall Club of Charleston remains a symbol of the millionaire's way of life.

Haunted House at 76 Meeting Street

In 1900 Daniel Ravenel bought the house at 76 Meeting Street in Charleston, and from the time of the purchase until the day he sold the dwelling he claimed the house was haunted. J. O. C. Tiedeman called on Ravenel in 1937 and asked him to explain why he believed his house was haunted. Ravenel told a dramatic story.

The house and the lot on which it stood were historic. The property was listed as Lot 214 on the Grand Modell of early Charleston, and at that time lay just inside the western wall of the original city. Known as the "Tan Yard," the lot very likely played a part in the large wild animal hide export business that developed in Charleston. In 1785 a house was built on the "Tan Yard" site.

The house is a typical Charleston single house, with wide piazzas facing south and a door opening from the piazza onto the street. Inside, a hall divides the front rooms from the others. As was customary in the old days, the drawing room was the front room on the second floor. The house is constructed of cypress and pine from the South Carolina Low Country forest. The quaint kitchen building is made of locally crafted brick and features a tiled roof. Due to the threat of fire in wooden outbuildings, the kitchen and servants' quarters were frequently constructed of brick and tile.

Judge Elihu Hale Bay, one of the home's original owners, was born in Havre de Grace, Maryland, and began his law practice in Pensacola, Florida, where, before the Revolution, he served as King's attorney. Bay received a certificate of citizenship in Charleston on February 18, 1784. He bought 76 Meeting Street shortly thereafter.

One evening about 1811, during a gathering in the drawing room, an altercation arose between two guests. The dispute became very heated and the two began to threaten a duel. The argument continued to rise and the men stomped up to the third floor and walked their paces. The duel in which they engaged was as real as any on a bluff overlooking the river, and the one at 76 Meeting Street resulted in a death.

Shortly after the burial of the man killed in the duel, the Bay family spoke of hearing footsteps that started on the third floor and continued to the stairway and on down to the drawing room on the second floor. When Daniel Ravenel bought the house he was warned about the footsteps, but he believed he could deal with a ghost.

The Ravenels used the room in which the duel had taken place as a guest room. On several occasions, guests reported being awakened suddenly during the night with the feeling that someone was in the room with them. Sometimes the large rocking chair in front of the fireplace rocked by itself.

Ravenel believed the ghost was the spirit of the man who had been killed in the duel, and he proceeded to play a trick on the ghost to get him to expose himself. He enlisted the help of a guest who was about to retire for the night in the haunted room. Daniel sprinkled some powder in the seat of the rocking chair. Sometime during the night the guest awoke to the sound of the chair rocking. He lit a lamp and examined the chair's seat. The powder was gone.

On another occasion, Ravenel was on the second floor piazza waiting for a family member to return from an evening out. Feeling tired he went into the front room and threw himself on the bed to rest. He must have fallen asleep, for the next thing he knew he was standing in the middle of the floor virtually scared to death. He claimed to be a man of calm and collected nature and not easily frightened, but in this instance he was scared stiff without any explanation for his terror.

One evening some time later, Ravenel came home to find two of his friends there awaiting his arrival. When the maid saw him come in, she remarked that she thought she had seen him go upstairs shortly before. He and his friends immediately grabbed what weapons of defense they could lay hands on and made a thorough search of the house, but found no one.

One morning, Ravenel came downstairs early, before daylight, to let in a servant. He noticed through the glass door someone sitting calmly on a sofa in the dining room. He switched on the light, but no one was there.

Daniel Ravenel sold 76 Meeting Street to the Vestry of St. Michael's Church in 1942 for use as a rectory. Since that time, there has been no report of a ghost.

The Day the Press Snitched on Charleston's Most Sacred Social Organization

On January 19, 1917, a Charleston newspaper printed a full account of the ball of the Saint Cecilia Society, the city's most sacred social organization. Never before in the history of the Saint Cecilia Society, which spanned a century and a half, had an account of one of its balls, and the names of those attending, been printed. The publication caused a great stir in the city. An editorial, said to have been written by John P. Grace, mayor of Charleston, appeared in the newspaper the following day. The editorial revealed something of Charleston's tradition—and something of Grace as well. The item was headed "The Saint Cecilia Ball," and a portion of it ran as follows:

> We carried on yesterday a full account of the Saint Cecilia ball. From the foundation of Charleston until the present moment, it has been regarded as an unwritten law that the annual events of this ancient society shall not be touched upon.
> Of course it was permissible for the 35,000 poor white people of Charleston to TALK about the Saint Cecilia, and to indulge in the thrilling sensation that comes to the proverbial cat when she looks at a queen. Some of them, moved by curiosity, even ventured within half a block of the Hibernian Hall to observe from afar the gay festivities.
> The press being forbidden to cover Saint Cecilia events, there grew up in the vulgar mind weird stories of what went on behind the scenes. While the Saint Cecilia has enjoyed the happy privilege of journalistic silence, it has therefore correspondingly suffered on the

tongue of gossip. The truth is that we always KNEW that the Saint Cecilia was just about the same as every other social collection of human beings—a little gayety flavored with a little frivolity; nothing more, nothing less. . . .

On January 17, 1964, the *New York Times* also reported on the Saint Cecilia Society and described the annual ball held at Hibernian Hall in Charleston thus:

The women did not wear hoop skirts and there were new wooden folding chairs in the 19th-century ballroom, but aside from that, the St. Cecilia Society's annual ball was like something out of "Gone With the Wind."

That newspaper went on to say that the Society, which shuns publicity and is rarely mentioned in local newspapers, is an aristocratic organization whose sole purpose is the giving of the annual ball. Its members are men, most of whose ancestors settled in Charleston nearly one hundred years before the American Revolution. They are what is left of the area's landed gentry, and although they can be exceedingly hospitable to strangers, they are unwilling to discuss Saint Cecilia. It has been explained that Charlestonians never left the room when the Saint Cecilia was mentioned, but they chose not to talk about it. Remaining silent about the Saint Cecilia was tradition.

The Saint Cecilia Society, named for the patron saint of music and musicians, was formally organized in 1762 for the purpose of presenting concerts for its members. Its members were wealthy plantation owners and good friends who had been giving amateur musicales off and on since 1737.

The first regular rules of the Society were printed in pamphlet form in 1774 with the following title page:

RULES
of the
ST. COECILIA SOCIETY,
Charlestown:
Printed, for the Society,
by Robert Wells,
MDCCLXXIV.

The pamphlet measured about three inches wide by six inches long, contained eleven pages, and was bound in board covers. The rules stipulated, among other provisions, that there would be annually four general meetings of the Society, namely, on Saint Coecilia's Day, which should also serve as the Society's anniversary, and on the third Thursday in February, May, and August, on which days the members should dine together. The Society members, on their anniversary, would elect by ballot a president, vice president, treasurer, and steward, and eleven other members, residents of Charleston who, with the forenamed officers, would be constituted managers for the current year.

The managers were empowered to set the number and times of the concerts. Any person desirous of becoming a member of the Saint Coecilia Society was required to signify same by a letter directed to the president of the Society. Then, when a vacancy occurred, the members present at the next general meeting had power to elect or reject the candidate. Election or rejection was by ballot only, and the assent of two-thirds of the members present was necessary for the admission of such candidate. Every person, on his election, was held accountable for subscribing to the rules of the Society, and paying to the treasurer for the use of the Society thirty-five pounds currency.

Until April, 1819, meetings and concerts were held at 9:00 PM on Thursdays. The first exception was during the Revolution when the city was under fire. Interruption of this ritual was a necessity. There is no mention of meetings during the time of the city's captivity, 1781 to 1786. The members were either in prison or riding with Francis Marion. Immediately upon the city's release, the Society met again and continued to do so regularly. In 1792 the managers wrote to Maj. Thomas Pinckney, then Minister to England, requesting he buy and send to them "one grand pianoforte and twenty pounds' worth of the best modern concert music."

The next exception to the Thursday night ritual came when Pres. James Monroe was a guest in Charleston in April 1819. Word of the lavish scenario of the president's travels reached Charleston before his arrival. In order that the president not set his foot on a green lawn or, at the worst, sandy soil at Prospect Hill Plantation in Georgetown County, a red carpet was laid from the canal to the entrance to the house, about two hundred yards away. The welcome of Monroe's party was equaled by the lavish departure the next morning on one of the plantation barges, profusely decorated and adorned for the occasion with the United States colors proudly flying at its head. Eight oarsmen dressed in ecru satin embellished with turquoise lace propelled the barge. When the president arrived in Charleston, the Saint Cecilia [the name corrupted from Saint Coecilia] gave a special concert and ball in his honor. This occurred on a Saturday. When President Washington visited Charleston in 1791 he had not been accorded those honors.

After President Monroe's visit, the concerts became less important and the dancing more so. By 1821 the group seems to have abandoned concerts altogether. Dates for the events were still as important as ever. When Mrs. St. Julien Ravenel mentioned the Saint Cecilia Society in 1906, she said, "Lent alone disturbs its dates; Saturday is unheard of; that would hardly be a real Saint Cecilia which did not begin on a Thursday at 9:00 PM." Three balls were given each season—the first in January and the second and third in February—carefully arranged to avoid touching upon Lent. Young ladies always came with a chaperone, and the greatest decorum prevailed. The newest bride present at the festivities was escorted to supper by the Society's president, and the others followed.

Managers controlled everything, entirely independent of feminine suggestion or assistance. The managers held themselves responsible for the pleasure and well-being of the guests. No lady was neglected; no stranger unwelcome. Not to attend the Saint Cecilia ball was to not be recognized in Charleston society. "If one is not eligible to the Saint Cecilia one simply is not a debutante," wrote one of the city's aristocrats about the elite club.

The Society owned its plate, damask, china, and glass, and a good stock of wine. The suppers were elegantly served, waited on by every butler and footman in town who could secure a swallow-tailed coat, grinning with delight when he recognized his acquaintances, especially his own "fambly."

The Society's first concerts were held at East Tradd Street, but fashion soon deserted that part of the town. For many years before 1860 the balls were given at St. Andrew's Hall, a handsome building on Broad Street. Invitations to the three annual supper dances were coveted.

In 1848 the invitation read

ST. CECILIA BALL
*The honor of your Company is requested at
St. Andrew's Hall, on Thursday Evening,
Feb. 3rd, at 8 o'clock.*

Wm. Ravenel, President
Charles Macbeth, Vice President
E. J. Porcher, Secy & treasurer
E. P. Milliken,   W. McKenzie Parker,
T. L. Wragg,   N. Barnwell,
Jan. 26th, 1848

In 1841 Wm. E. Vanderhorst of Chapel Street received an invitation that read

ST. CECILIA BALL
*The Honor of Your Company is Requested at
St. Andrews Hall, on Thursday Evening, the
18th February.*

MANAGERS
James L. Petigru, President
Henry A. Middleton, Vice-President
T. L. Wragg, Secretary and Treasurer.
E. P. Milliken,   Dr. M. C. King
Dr. E. H. Heas,   Charles McBeth
Charleston, Feb. 11, 1841

The dances were card dances, and the order of dances and engagements on A. S. Salley's card on February 11, 1841, read

1. Quadrille.   Lidie Heyward
2. Waltz.   Miss Nellie Hazlehurst
3. Quadrille.   Mrs. Poffenhein Ravenel
4. Waltz.   Miss Lizzie Boykin
5. Polka Glide.   Miss Meta Smyth

6. Quadrille.	Miss Bessie Ravenel
7. Deux Temps.	Miss Lizzie Valk
8. Quadrille.	Miss Fannie Perry
9. Waltz.	Miss Mattie Valk
10. Quadrille.	Miss Randolph
11. Deux Temps.	Miss Annie Inglesby
12. Quadrille.	Miss Nina Randolph
PROMINADE—SUPPER	Miss Lizzie Valk
13. Waltz.	Miss May Paine
14. Polka Glide.	Miss Lizzie Parker
15. Waltz.	Miss Louise Chisolm
16. Waltz.	Miss Adele Hayne

In later years, the Saint Cecilia Society balls were held in the second floor ballroom of the Hibernian Hall on Meeting Street. Ball goers represented such famous French Huguenot families as the Gaillards, Hugers, Legares, Manigaults, Prioleaus, Ravenels, and the Huguenins. English families were the Rutledges, Heywards, Middletons, Holmeses, Cheveses, and Simonses. No one has ever been expelled from the organization, the mere threat being enough to bring about desired deportment.

"There were two families. . . . ," said Jack Leland, former managing editor of the Charleston *Post and Courier.* "One came from Florida during World War I. They were in construction. That was all right, but then they got into bootlegging and began to associate with the Charleston Mafia. When a daughter desired to make her debut and be presented at the St. Cecilia, there was some question. A debut list was made each year, and the secretary was employed to keep that list. Well, in order to prevent that girl from making her debut, there was no debut list that season. That was Charleston's way of saying . . .

"A farmer came to town during World War II and bought some oil delivery trucks. He married an Alabama girl and became a millionaire. Their daughters made debuts, alongside Old Charleston."

In 1964 the ball was typical of those held in recent years. Fires burned in the four fireplaces in the ballroom on the second floor of Hibernian Hall. Almost everything except the lace curtains was banked in southern smilax.

Anyone held up in the traffic jam on Meeting Street, viewed

men in white gloves and their formally clad wives and daughters, all a-hurry to reach the front door of Hibernian Hall. There were sixteen dances and two extras, one at the beginning and one after the midnight supper. Men kept their gloves on except during the meal. No man cut in on another while dancing, and smoking on the dance floor was prohibited. Mocha punch, made with coffee, chocolate, cream, ice, and a mild wine, was the strongest of the beverages.

Edward Wittstein and his orchestra came from New Haven to play at the 1964 ball, as they had done for more than thirty years. Many of the selections were from George Gershwin's folk opera *Porgy and Bess*, based on the book *Porgy* by Charlestonian DuBose Heyward.

At the stroke of midnight, Nathaniel L. Barnwell, Jr., president of the Society, led the Grand March, escorting the Bride of the Ball around the dance floor. The midnight supper included breast of chicken with almonds and wild rice, spiced peaches, sugar peas with mushrooms, fruit salad with cottage cheese, lemon sponge cake, and coffee.

It is true that the Society columns appearing in Charleston newspapers today rarely print the names of the city's true aristocrats. Like the Charleston earthquakes, they have enjoyed the happy privilege of journalistic silence. But the paper that snitched on the blue bloods' Saint Cecilia Society in 1917 made the point that they believed it perfectly legitimate for the newspaper, which represented *all* classes of people, to report on the event. Mr. Grace believed that because he was not present at the Saint Cecilia ball he maintained the freedom to report it. One wonders, though, if Mayor Grace had been invited to the ball, would he have considered the publication of a story on it in good taste?

SALADS

Marinated Asparagus

1 can white asparagus spears, drained
1/4 cup apple cider vinegar
1/4 cup vegetable oil
water
1 teaspoon chopped chives or minced green onion tops, for garnish

Place asparagus in a shallow dish. Add vinegar, oil, and enough water to cover spears. Marinate in refrigerator overnight. Drain asparagus and serve on lettuce. Garnish with a sprinkle of chives or onion and a few drops of the marinade. Serves 4.

Cucumber Salad

1 package lime Jell-O
3/4 cup boiling water
1 cup mayonnaise
2 3-ounce packages cream cheese (room temperature)
2 tablespoons lemon juice
3/4 cup grated unpeeled cucumber, drained and squeezed
(about 2 medium or 1-1/2 very large)
1/4 cup finely chopped onion

Dissolve Jell-O in water. Cool slightly. Stir in mayonnaise, cream cheese, and lemon juice and beat until smooth with hand beater or electric mixer. Let chill until slightly thickened. Stir in cucumber and onion. Pour into mold. Serves 8.

Tomato Aspic

1 can stewed tomatoes
1 package lemon Jell-O
2 tablespoons wine vinegar
dash Tobasco sauce

Bring tomatoes to a boil. While boiling, add Jell-O, vinegar, and Tobasco. Cool and chill. Serves 8.
[NOTE: Serves well in halved orange peels.]

Spinach Salad

1 egg, beaten slightly
1/4 cup vegetable oil
juice of 1 lemon
1 tablespoon Parmesan cheese
1 tablespoon Dijon mustard
1 teaspoon sugar
1 teaspoon Worcestershire sauce
1/2 teaspoon salt
1/8 teaspoon black pepper
1 bunch fresh spinach
4 medium-sized fresh mushrooms
1 slice bacon, fried and crumbled
2 hard-boiled eggs, sliced

Blend first nine ingredients together. Store in refrigerator until needed. Makes 1 cup. Pull spinach into pieces and put in large salad bowl. Cover with dressing. Garnish with mushrooms, eggs, and bacon. Serves 4.

Marinated Tomatoes

1/2 cup wine vinegar
1/4 cup water
1 tablespoon sugar
2 teaspoons grated onion
freshly ground black pepper, to taste
4 tomatoes, sliced

Combine first 5 ingredients and pour over tomatoes. Marinate in freezer until icy. Serves 6.

Spaghetti Salad

1 pound spaghetti noodles
1/2 16-ounce bottle Catalina dressing
3/4 8-ounce bottle herb and garlic salad dressing
1/2 16-ounce bottle French dressing
1/2 8-ounce bottle Italian dressing
1 teaspoon celery seed
2 large tomatoes, cut into small wedges
1 cucumber, shredded or chopped
1 medium onion, chopped

Cook spaghetti noodles as directed on package. Wash well with cold water. Chill about 2 hours. Combine all dressings and mix well. Stir in celery seed. In a large bowl, place 3/4 of the spaghetti; cover with dressings and mix well. Stir in remaining noodles. Add tomato, cucumber, and onion and mix well. Chill until ready to serve. Serves 6.

Vinegar Salad

4 envelopes (1 box) unflavored gelatin
2 pints water
1 10-ounce jar Maraschino cherries
1/2 cup apple cider vinegar
1 16-ounce can crushed pineapple, drained
1 dozen sweet midget pickles, cut into small pieces
1 cup chopped nuts
1-1/2 cups sugar
1 teaspoon whole cloves
mayonnaise, for garnish
lettuce

Soak gelatin in 1 pint cold water. To the second pint of water, add cloves and boil three minutes; strain and add dissolved gelatin. Stir in sugar, vinegar, and pineapple juice. When mixture begins to stiffen, add fruit, nuts, and pickles. Serve on lettuce with mayonnaise. Good with ham or chicken. Serves 30.

Strawberry Salad

3 packages strawberry Jello-O
1 cup boiling water
1 16-ounce can crushed pineapple
2 packages frozen strawberries, thawed
1 cup broken nuts
1 cup mashed banana
2 16-ounce cartons sour cream

Dissolve Jell-O in water. Combine remaining ingredients and add to Jell-O. Put one-half mixture in 9-by-12-inch glass dish. Place in refrigerator until congealed. When congealed, spread sour cream on top and add remaining Jell-O mixture. Return to refrigerator. Cut into large squares and serve on lettuce. Serves 8.
[NOTE: You may use two packages of Jell-O and drain strawberries and pineapple. In order to take advantage of the fruit juice, I use three packages of Jell-O and do not drain the fruit.]

Heavenly Orange Fluff

2 packages orange Jell-O
2 cups hot water
1 small can frozen orange juice, undiluted
2 cans Mandarin oranges, drained
1 8-ounce can crushed pineapple

Dissolve gelatin in water. Stir in orange juice. Cool. Add Mandarin oranges and pineapple to gelatin mixture. Pour into 13-by-11-inch dish. Place in refrigerator to congeal.

TOPPING

1 package instant lemon pudding
1 cup milk
1/2 pint whipping cream

Beat pudding with milk until slightly firm. Whip cream and fold into pudding. Spread on top of congealed salad. Cut into squares and serve on lettuce. Serves 15.

Orange Jell-O

1 large package orange Jell-O
1 package unflavored gelatin
2 cups hot water
1 cup miniature marshmallows
1 pint orange sherbet
1 16-ounce can crushed pineapple
1/2 cup chopped nuts
1 large carton Cool Whip
2 cans Mandarin oranges, drained

Dissolve Jell-O and gelatin in water. Chill until slightly thickened. Stir in remaining ingredients. Refrigerate until completely congealed. Serves 8.

Connoisseur
Congealed Salad

2 packages lemon Jell-O
2 cups boiling water
2 cups 7-Up
2 large bananas, sliced
1 20-ounce can crushed pineapple, drained (reserve juice)
1 cup miniature marshmallows

Dissolve Jell-O in water. Cool. Add 7-Up. Refrigerate until slightly syrupy. Add pineapple, bananas, and marshmallows. Pour into 9-by-13-inch pan. Chill until firm. Serves 8.

TOPPING

1 cup pineapple juice
1/2 cup sugar
1 egg yolk, well beaten
2 tablespoons all-purpose flour
1 cup whipping cream, whipped
Cracker Barrel sharp cheddar and Parmesan cheese, grated, for garnish

Mix flour and sugar together. Blend in juice and egg. Cook over low heat, stirring until thickened. Cool completely. Fold in whipped cream. Spread over fruited gelatin. Sprinkle with cheese. Cut into squares to serve. Serves 8.

Ginger Ale Salad

1 package lime Jell-O
1/2 cup hot water
1 cup ginger ale
1 16-ounce can sliced peaches
1/2 cup chopped celery
1/2 cup mixed nuts

Dissolve Jell-O in hot water. Stir in ginger ale, peaches, celery, and nuts. Place in refrigerator until congealed. Serves 8.

Cranberry Salad

1 pound cranberries, ground or crushed, or 1 can cranberry
sauce
rind of 1 orange, grated
2 packages red Jell-O (raspberry and cherry)
1 cup water
1 cup sugar
1 8-ounce can crushed pineapple
1/2 cup chopped pecans

Bring water to boil and dissolve Jell-O. Add other ingredients. Refrigerator until firm. Serves 8.

Congealed Fruit Salad

1 8-ounce package cream cheese (room temperature)
4 tablespoons mayonnaise
juice of 1 lemon
1/8 teaspoon salt
2/3 cup whipping cream, whipped
1/2 cup Maraschino cherries, chopped
1 8-ounce can crushed pineapple

Mix cream cheese and mayonnaise until smooth. Add lemon juice, salt, and whipped cream; blend well. Stir in cherries and pineapple. Freeze 3 hours. Serves 8.

Georgia Peach Salad

1 cup boiling water
2 3-ounce packages peach Jell-O
3 teaspoons prepared horseradish
1 cup mayonnaise
1 cup small curd cottage cheese
2 cups crushed pineapple
1 14-ounce can Eagle Brand condensed milk
1 cup chopped nuts

Dissolve Jell-O in water. Stir in horseradish and pour into blender. Add mayonnaise and blend well. Add cottage cheese, pineapple, milk, and nuts. Pour into Pyrex dish and chill until firm. Serves 8.

Aunt Lill's
Apricot Acapulco

1 3-ounce package cream cheese (reserve 1/4 for dressing)
1 teaspoon apricot syrup
1 teaspoon pineapple syrup
1/2 teaspoon lemon juice
1 tablespoon sugar
3 tablespoons ground, toasted almonds
3 tablespoons chopped red maraschino cherries
1 1-pound can whole peeled apricots
9 slices canned pineapple
2 bananas
lettuce

Mix together all ingredients except apricots, pineapple, and bananas. Remove seeds from apricots and stuff with above mixture. Press halves back together and place a stuffed apricot in the center of each pineapple slice. Place on platter of lettuce. When ready to serve, slice bananas and arrange pieces around the salad. Serve with the following dressing. Serves 8.

DRESSING

1/2 cup mayonnaise
reserved cream cheese
1 teaspoon apricot syrup
1 teaspoon pineapple syrup
1/2 teaspoon lemon juice
1/4 teaspoon paprika
1/8 teaspoon salt

Combine ingredients and beat until smooth.

Watermelon Fruit Salad

1 medium-sized oblong watermelon
crushed ice
2 cantaloupes, scooped out into balls
1 16-ounce can pineapple chunks
1 small jar maraschino cherries
1 cup fresh blueberries

Cut watermelon in half and scoop meat out in balls. Cut edge of rind in points. Use each half for a bowl. Place crushed ice in bowl until time to use. Cover with waxed paper. When ready to use, empty bowls and fill with watermelon and cantaloupe balls, chunks of pineapple, and maraschino cherries. Top with blueberries. Serves 20.

Sweet Dressing for Fruit Salad

1 tablespoon prepared mustard
1 teaspoon salt
1 teaspoon grated onion
2 tablespoons white vinegar
1 teaspoon paprika
1 tablespoon celery salt
1/3 cup honey
1 cup vegetable oil

Using a hand whisk, beat together first seven ingredients. Slowly add oil, beating just until blended well. Do not use blender. Yields about 1-1/2 cups.

DESSERTS

"Raving Good" Presbyterian Gingerbread

2 cups butter or margarine, softened
1 cup sugar
1 egg
1 cup molasses ("Grandma's" brand)
2-1/4 cups all-purpose flour
1-1/2 teaspoons baking soda
1/2 teaspoon salt
1 teaspoon ground cinnamon
1 teaspoon ground ginger
1 cup hot water
lemon rind strips to garnish
maraschino cherries to garnish

Beat butter at medium speed, gradually adding sugar, until fluffy. Add egg and molasses, mixing well. Combine flour, soda, salt, cinnamon, and ginger; add to creamed mixture alternately with water, beginning and ending with flour mixture. Mix well after each addition. Pour batter into lightly greased and floured 13-by-9-by-2-inch pan Bake at 350 degrees for 35 to 40 minutes, until toothpick inserted comes out clean. Serve with lemon sauce. Garnish with lemon rind strips and a cherry.

LEMON SAUCE

1/2 cup butter or margarine
1 cup sugar
1/4 cup water
1 egg, beaten
juice and grated rind of 1 lemon

Melt butter in saucepan over medium heat. Add remaining ingredients. stirring constantly. Continue cooking until mixture reaches 169 degrees.

Aunt Lill's
Lemon Tea Cakes

CRUST

1 cup butter, melted
2 cups all-purpose flour, sifted
1/2 cup confectioners sugar

Mix all ingredients together and spread evenly in a greased 9-by-13-inch pan. Bake at 350 degrees for 15 minutes, while preparing topping.

TOPPING

2 cups sugar
4 tablespoons all-purpose flour
1 teaspoon baking powder
4 eggs
1/4 teaspoon salt
6 tablespoons lemon juice
confectioners sugar to garnish

Combine sugar, flour, and baking powder. Mix in eggs, one at a time, beating after each. Add salt and lemon juice.

Remove crust from oven and cover with topping. Bake at 350 degrees for 25 minutes. When done, sprinkle with confectioners sugar. Cool and cut into squares. Makes about 3 dozen.

Aunt Lill's
Lemon Lucerne

1 cup sugar
2 tablespoons cornstarch
1/8 teaspoon salt
1 cup water
1/4 cup lemon juice
grated rind of 1 lemon
1 egg, lightly beaten
1 teaspoon vanilla extract
1 cup heavy cream, whipped

Combine sugar, cornstarch, and salt; blend in water. Cook over medium heat, stirring constantly, until thickened. Add lemon juice. Stir a small amount of the hot mixture into beaten egg. Stir egg into remaining hot mixture. Cook gently, stirring constantly, for 3 minutes. Remove from heat. Add rind and vanilla. Cool 10 minutes. Fold in whipped cream and spoon into individual serving dishes. May be topped with whipped cream. Serves 12.

Sid's Blueberry Cobbler

3 cups fresh blueberries
1 8-ounce can crushed pineapple, drained
1 box Duncan Hines white cake mix
1/2 stick butter

Fill 8-by-8-inch Pyrex dish with blueberries to about 1-1/2 inches from top. Cover with pineapple. Spread cake mix over the pineapple. Mash cake mix down into fruit. Dot with butter. Bake at 350 degrees until the top browns.

Orange Coconut Balls

1 stick margarine
1 box confectioners sugar
1 small can frozen orange juice, undiluted
4 cups crushed vanilla wafers
2 cups coconut

Mix margarine and powdered sugar. Add forzen orange juice. Stir in vanilla wafers and form into balls. Roll balls in coconut.

Raspberry Ice Cream

1 3-ounce package raspberry flavored gelatin
1/2 cup boiling water
1 10-ounce package fresh raspberries, or frozen berries, thawed
2 eggs, beaten
1 cup whipping cream
1 package instant vanilla pudding
2/3 cup sugar
2 teaspoons vanilla extract
1 quart milk

In mixing bowl, dissolve gelatin in boiling water and stir in fruit. In separate bowl mix eggs, whipping cream, pudding, sugar, and vanilla; stir into gelatin. Pour mixture into 1-gallon ice cream freezer container. Add milk and stir until blended. Freeze according to freezer manufacturer's directions. Make 2 quarts.
[Other fruit may be substituted for raspberries.]

Island Ice Cream Odyssey

1 fresh pineapple
1 8-ounce carton plain yogurt
2 bananas, peeled
5 packets Sweet 'N Low
1/4 cup honey

Use 1-quart Donvier ice cream freezer that requires no ice, no salt, and no electricity. Place the Donvier cylinder in the freezer for 24 hours before using. It is important to thoroughly freeze the Chillfast aluminum cylinder.

To prepare pineapple, cut off top. To remove the meat from the peel, cut a 1-inch incision in side of pineapple about 1 inch from bottom and maneuver knife gently back and forth and around until the pineapple meat has been sliced through, without puncturing the peel. After the pineapple meat has been severed from the bottom, cut a full circle inside the peel from the top, down to the place where it has been previously cut, to loosen the meat. Cut pineapple meat into four sections and pull each section out of peel, leaving the pineapple peel intact.

Cut away the core of the pineapple sections and discard. Coarsely chop the pineapple meat and put in Cuisinart. Add bananas and process 10 seconds. Add Sweet 'N Low and honey and process 5 seconds. Scrape sides of Cuisinart bowl, add yogurt and process 5 seconds. Mixture should be the consistency of a milk shake. If not, mix a bit longer. Remove Donvier cylinder from freezer and fit the bottom of the blade in the shallow hole at the bottom of the cylinder. Pour in the mixed ingredients. Place the lid on the cylinder, carefully aligning the marks on the cylinder ring with the lock tab on the lid. Lock the lid by turning it counterclockwise into position. Hold the case handle with one hand and attach the handle, turning it clockwise slowly 3 or 4 times. Let the mixture sit for 2 to 3 minutes, then turn the handle clockwise again 2 or 3 times. Turn handle occasionally for 20 minutes, to prevent ice cream from sticking to the sides. Remove the dasher from the cylinder and place cylinder in freezer for a couple hours. When ice cream is firm, spoon it into the pineapple shell and wrap with Saran Wrap. Place in freezer for 24 hours. Just before serving, slice the pineapple lengthwise and cut each side into 10 wedge-shaped servings. Two wedges make one dessert. Serves 5.
[This dessert is very low in calories and fat content.]

CANDIES

Strawberries

2 packages strawberry Jell-O
1 8-ounce can sweetened condensed milk
1/2 cup chopped pecans
1 can flaked coconut
1 teaspoon vanilla extract
1/2 teaspoon salt
red colored sugar, for garnish
green colored slivered almonds, for garnish

Mix first six ingredients together and chill for a few hours. Shape into strawberries. Roll in sugar and insert almond on each for stem.

Sour Cream Fudge

2 cups granulated sugar
1 cup confectioners sugar
1 cup sour cream
3 squares unsweetened chocolate
1/4 teaspoon salt
1 teaspoon vanilla extract
1 tablespoon butter
1 cup chopped nuts

Mix sugars, sour cream, chocolate, and salt in a heavy saucepan and bring to a boil over medium heat, stirring occasionally. Reduce heat and cook without stirring until small ball forms when mixture is dropped into cold water (234 degrees on candy thermometer). Add butter and vanilla and cool to lukewarm. Add nuts and beat until mixture loses its gloss. Pour into greased 8-inch square pan. Allow to cool until firm. Cut into squares.

Uncooked Fudge

4 cups confectioners sugar
4 tablespoons butter
3 squares baking chocolate
1/4 cup evaporated milk
1/4 teaspoon salt
1 teaspoon vanilla extract
1/2 cup chopped pecans or walnuts

Melt butter and chocolate together in double boiler. Mix sugar and milk until smooth; add chocolate mixture and work until well blended. Add salt, vanilla, and nuts. Press into buttered pan. Cut into squares.

PIES & PUDDINGS

Pecan Chiffon Pie

makes 2 pies

1 cup coarsely chopped pecans
1 cup dark brown sugar
1-1/3 cups plus 2 tablespoons water
4 tablespoons cornstarch
1/4 cup water
2/3 cup egg whites (room temperature)
1/4 cup sugar
2 baked 8-inch pie shells
1/2 pint whipping cream

Spread pecans on baking sheet and bake at 250–275 degrees for 10 minutes or until nuts begin to brown. (To test, take out a few, let them cool, and taste them. The toasted nuts will have a more pronounced, nutty flavor.) Combine brown sugar and 1-1/3 plus 2 tablespoons water; bring to a boil over medium heat. Mix together cornstarch and 1/4 cup water; add to boiling brown sugar mixture. Continue cooking, stirring constantly with a whisk, until mixture becomes clear and is the consistency of a thick pudding; remove from heat. Whip egg whites at high speed with electric mixer until peaks form. Slowly add granulated sugar and continue beating until peaks are stiff. Reduce mixer speed to low and gently add the hot brown sugar mixture and nuts. (Reserve a few nuts for garnish.) As soon as everything is blended, turn off mixer. Do not overmix. Pile filling lightly into baked pie shells.

Before serving, whip cream until stiff; divide and spread over cooled pies. Sprinkle finely chopped reserved pecans over top for garnish.

Pecan Pie

**3 eggs
1 cup light brown sugar
1 cup white Karo syrup
1 cup pecans
1 unbaked 9-inch pie shell**

Beat eggs until foamy. Add sugar and syrup and continue beating until well mixed. Pour mixture into pie shell. Sprinkle pecans over filling and bake at 325 degrees for one hour.

CRUST

**1 cup all-purpose flour
1/2 cup shortening
1/2 cup cold water**

Cut shortening into flour and add water. Form into ball, flatten, and roll out with rolling pin. Press into 9-inch pie pan. Trim edges.

Maraschino Soufflé Pie

1 18-ounce jar red maraschino cherries
1 8-1/2-ounce can crushed pineapple
water
1 envelope unflavored gelatin
4 beaten egg yolks
2 tablespoons lemon juice
1/8 teaspoon salt
4 egg whites
1/2 cup sugar
1/2 cup heavy cream
coconut pie shell

Drain cherries and chop. (Set aside a few whole cherries for garnish.) Drain pineapple, reserving syrup. Add enough water to pineapple syrup to make 3/4 cup liquid. Soften gelatin in the liquid; add egg yolks. Blend and stir constantly over low heat until gelatin dissolves and mixture coats a metal spoon, about 5 minutes. Remove from heat and stir in lemon juice and salt. Cool. Add cherries and pineapple. Beat egg whites until soft peaks form. Gradually add sugar, beating until stiff but not dry. Fold egg whites into mixture of gelatin. Beat cream until soft peaks form; fold into gelatin mixture. Spread mixture in pie shell and chill about 4 hours. Garnish with whole cherries.

Coconut Pie Shell

1/2 cup butter
1 3-1/2-ounce can flaked coconut

Melt butter in large skillet over medium heat. Add coconut and toss until evenly coated. Press mixture evenly and firmly on bottom and sides of pie plate. Form a rim around plate. Cover sides and rim of shell with strips of aluminum foil. Bake at 300 degrees for 20 minutes or until bottom of shell starts to brown. Remove foil and bake 10 minutes longer. Chill.

Two-Crust Cherry Pie

CRUST

2 cups all-purpose flour, sifted
1-1/2 teaspoons salt
1/2 cup shortening
1/4 cup ice water

Combine flour and salt. Cut in shortening. Add water; mix with a fork until all flour is moistened. Press dough firmly together into a ball; divide in half. Roll one half into a thin crust and ease into a 9-inch pie pan. Trim ragged edges with scissors, leaving 1/2-inch hanging over edge of pan. Fold overhanging pastry up to form a high fluted edge—to hold a generous amount of filling. Hook pastry under rim of pan at several points to help prevent shrinking during baking.

FILLING

2 cans pitted cherries
1-1/2 cups all-purpose flour
1 cup sugar
1/4 teaspoon lemon extract
1/4 teaspoon almond extract
1/4 teaspoon red food coloring
2 tablespoons butter

Drain cherries; reserve juice. Mix flour and sugar. Stir in 1 cup cherry juice, extract, and food coloring. Cook until thick, stirring constantly. Add butter. Place cherries in pastry shell; pour mixture over cherries. Roll out remaining dough; cut into strips. Arrange strips like lattice work over pie. Sprinkle lattice with a little sugar. Cover pie with aluminum foil and bake at 425 degrees for 10 minutes. Remove foil; reduce heat to 350 degrees and continue baking for 45 minutes.

Key Lime Pie

1 9-inch baked pie shell
1 15-ounce can sweetened condensed milk
1 tablespoon grated lemon peel
1/2 teaspoon grated lime peel
1/4 cup fresh lime juice
1/4 cup fresh lemon juice
3 drops green food coloring
3 eggs, separated
1/4 teaspoon cream of tartar
1/4 cup shredded coconut

Blend milk, fruit peel, juices, and food coloring. Beat egg yolks slightly and blend into juice mixture; set aside. Beat egg whites and cream of tartar until stiff and glossy; fold gently into lemon-lime mixture. Pile into pie shell. Chill several hours until set. Sprinkle coconut over top before serving.

Island Pie

2 eggs, beaten
1 cup plus 2 tablespoons sugar
1/2 cup all-purpose flour
1 stick butter, melted
1 teaspoon vanilla extract
1 cup chocolate chips
1 cup chopped English walnuts
1 9-inch unbaked pie shell

Blend all ingredients together. Pour into pie shell and bake 30 minutes at 350 degrees.

Hell Hole Swamp Mud Pie

18 chocolate wafers, crushed
1/3 cup melted butter
2 squares unsweetened chocolate
1/2 cup sugar
1 tablespoon butter
1 small can evaporated milk
1 quart coffee ice cream
1 cup whipping cream (optional)
1/2 cup chopped nuts (optional)

Combine crushed wafers and melted butter; press into 9-inch pie pan, covering bottom and sides. Chill overnight.

Melt chocolate over hot water; stir in sugar and one tablespoon butter. Add milk slowly. Cook over hot water (medium heat), stirring occasionally, until thick. Cool to room temperature.

Fill pie shell with softened coffee ice cream (soft enough to spread easily). Pour cool fudge sauce over ice cream and freeze.

OPTION: At serving time, whip cream and spread on top. Sprinkle with chopped nuts.
• *Personally, I leave these off. The dessert is fabulous without them.*
NR

It's-A-Sin
Strawberry Pudding

1 1-pound box vanilla wafers, crushed
1 stick butter
1-1/2 cups confectioners sugar
2 eggs
1 quart strawberries
1/2 pint whipping cream, whipped

Spread half of wafer crumbs in bottom of 2-quart dish. Cream butter and sugar. Add eggs, beating thoroughly. Mix berries, whipped cream, egg batter, and the remaining crumbs; spread in dish. Refrigerate overnight.

Persimmon Pudding

1 cup persimmon pulp
1-1/2 cups milk
1 egg
1/3 stick butter, melted
1-1/2 cups sugar
1-3/4 cups sifted all-purpose flour
1/2 teaspoon baking soda
1/2 teaspoon baking powder
1/2 teaspoon salt
1/2 teaspoon cinnamon
1/4 teaspoon nutmeg

Wash persimmons and press through a sieve. Mix pulp, milk, egg, and butter. Stir in dry ingredients. Pour into a 8-by-8-inch baking dish. Bake at 325 degrees for 1 hour.

A Boy's Story of His Ma's Christmas Cake

Sugar, butter, raisins, eggs,
Almonds, cherries, ground nutmegs,
Candied lemon peel and dates—
Products of our various states;

All these things went into it:
Mama's fruit cake, bit by bit.
Then she baked it nice and brown
As some friends of mine dropped round—

Naughty boys with whom I run,
Thinking they would have some fun.
"Let's give it a drink of rum,"
Said one boy, "Well, I have some."

O'er the cake the flask he tipped—
Oh, my gosh! the bottle slipped!
And the fruit cake got it all
Just as I heard Mama call:

"Boys, I want you to help me—
Get the tin cake box," said she.
"Then we'll put the cake away
To be kept 'till Chrismas Day."

Oh, we did the job up right
Then clamped on the lid real tight!
At this thing we were adept,
And in ignorance Ma was kept.

Now that cake was really moist
When at Christmas we rejoiced!
"'Tis the best one yet," said Dad.
Cried my Ma, "I am so glad."

She had cut me a thick slice
Then she served me again twice,
But I snitched another piece~
I was having quite a feast.

By this time I felt quite "woozy,"
For that cake was really "boozy".
When another piece I took,
Ma gave me a dirty look.

But I held the slice up high,
Addressed Dad and winked my eye:
"Let us drink a toast with this
To dear Mama's health and bliss."

"You can't drink with that," said Ma.
"Ah, that's what you think," cried Da.
Then we toasted Ma, and I
By this time was really high.

Ma, not knowing what to think
Sermonized against strong drink.
"Ma," I said, "for pity's sake
I got drunk on your fruit cake."

                    ~by Lillian M. Dunn ("Aunt Lill")

CAKES

Sideboard Buttermilk Pound Cake

3 cups sugar
3 cups all-purpose or cake flour
5 large eggs (room temperature)
1 stick margarine or butter, softened
1/2 cup shortening
1 cup buttermilk
1 teaspoon vanilla extract
1 teaspoon lemon extract
1 teaspoon almond extract

Cream sugar, margarine, and shortening thoroughly. Add eggs, one at a time, blending well. Add flour and buttermilk alternately, mixing thoroughly after each addition. Add flavorings. Pour into tube pan that has been sprayed with Pam. Bake at 350 degrees for 1 hour and 15 minutes. Cool in pan about 20 minutes.

Sour Cream Pound Cake

2 sticks butter, softened
3 cups sugar
6 large eggs
3 cups cake flour
1/4 teaspoon soda
1 cup sour cream
2 teaspoons vanilla extract
1/2 teaspoon lemon extract
1/4 teaspoon almond extract
1/4 teaspoon orange extract

Cream butter and sugar. Add eggs, alternating with flour that has been sifted 3 times with soda. Stir in sour cream and flavorings. Bake in greased bundt or tube pan 1-1/2 hours at 300 degrees.

Charleston's
Lady Baltimore Cake

A Christmas delicacy made famous long ago by cooks of the coastal South Carolina and Georgia plantation mansions. Lady Baltimore cakes were always offered on the menu at Charleston's Lady Baltimore Tea Room. Owen Wister, U. S. novelist, immortalized this cake in his book Lady Baltimore. My thanks to Christian Frinck, instructor at Johnson & Wales University, for teaching me to make this particular cake.

3/4 cup butter
1-1/2 cups sugar
1 tablespoon vanilla extract
1/2 tablespoon almond extract
1 cup milk
4 tablespoons baking powder
1/4 tablespoon salt
3 cups cake flour, sifted
4 eggs

Cream butter until very fluffy and add sugar slowly. Continue creaming at medium speed until the mixture is like whipped cream. Turn off mixer. Add flavorings to milk. Sift baking powder, salt, and flour together four times. With mixer on lowest speed, add dry ingredients to cream mixture alternately with milk, ending with the dry mixture. When blended well, add eggs, one at a time, beating at low speed. Mix until smooth. Pour batter into 3 greased and floured 9-inch layer cake pans. Bake at 350 degrees for 30 minutes. Cool in pans for 15 minutes. Remove to wire racks.

FILLING

2 cups raisins
2 cups pecan pieces
12 figs
3 tablespoons brandy or sherry (optional)

Cut figs and raisins finely and add to pecan pieces. Add brandy or sherry and let stand 1 hour or more.

Make a double recipe of Lady Baltimore Frosting (page 178). Stir 1/3 of the frosting mix into the filling. Stack bottom 2 layers, spreading filling on top of each. Place remaining layer on top. Spread balance of frosting generously on top and sides of cake. [When a cake is properly frosted, no part of any layer shows through the frosting. In order to prevent cake crumbs from becoming mixed with frosting, wash and thoroughly dry spatula frequently during the frosting process.]

Indulgent Red Velvet Cake

1 box white cake mix
1 box instant chocolate pudding
2 cups milk
2 eggs
1 small bottle red food coloring
1/4 cup vegetable oil
1 tablespoon apple cider vinegar
1 teaspoon baking soda

Combine cake mix, pudding, milk, eggs, food coloring, and oil; mix well. Dissolve soda in vinegar and stir into batter. Pour into 3 greased 9-inch round cake pans and bake at 350 degrees for 25 minutes.

ICING

1 stick butter, softened
1 8-ounce package cream cheese, softened
1 box confectioners sugar
1 teaspoon vanilla extract

Whip butter and cream cheese until fluffy. Add confectioners sugar gradually, beating until smooth and creamy. Stir in vanilla and spread between layers and over top and sides of cooled cake.

Chocolate Chips
Pound Cake

1 box Duncan Hines yellow or white cake mix
1 small package instant vanilla pudding
1 cup water
1 cup vegetable oil
4 eggs
1 6-ounce package chocolate chips
1 bar sweet German chocolate, grated

Combine all ingredients except chocolate; beat well. Carefully fold in chocolate. Bake in bundt pan 60 minutes at 350 degrees. Cool in pan 1-1/2 hours. Invert on cake plate.

Chocolate Chip Cake

1 package instant vanilla pudding
1 package Duncan Hines white cake mix
1 cup water
1 cup vegetable oil
4 eggs
1 6-ounce package tiny chocolate chips
1 bar German chocolate, grated

Combine all ingredients except chocolate and beat well. Carefully fold in chocolate chips and two-thirds of the grated chocolate. Bake in bundt pan for 1 hour at 350 degrees. Remove from oven immediately. Sprinkle remaining one-third chocolate over top. Leave in pan for 1-1/3 hours. Remove from pan. Set upright on plate so chocolate is on top.

Marble Top Cake

1 package yellow cake mix
2/3 cup water
2/3 cup vegetable oil
1 box instant vanilla pudding
4 eggs
2/3 cup Smucker's hot fudge topping or **Hershey's chocolate syrup**

Mix together top four ingredients. When well blended, beat in eggs one at a time. Pour two-thirds of batter in greased bundt pan. Mix remaining batter with chocolate syrup. Pour on top. Bake 1 hour at 350 degrees. Cool in pan 15 minutes.

Threefold Chocolate Cake

1 box instant chocolate pudding
1 box chocolate or **devil's food cake mix**
1-3/4 cups milk
2 eggs
1 12-ounce package chocolate chips
1/2 cup chopped nuts

Combine pudding mix, cake mix, milk, and eggs in bowl. Mix by hand until well blended or 2 minutes on low with electric mixer. Stir in chips and nuts. Pour into greased and floured bundt pan. Bake at 350 degrees for 55 minutes. Cool for 15 minutes in pan.

Spicy Raisin Coffee Cake

1/2 cup margarine
1 cup sugar
2 eggs
1 teaspoon vanilla extract
1 cup sour cream
1 teaspoon baking soda
2 cups sifted all-purpose flour
1/2 teaspoon baking powder
1/4 teaspoon salt
1-1/2 cups raisins
1 cup chopped English walnuts or pecans
1/2 cup sugar
1 teaspoon cinnamon

Cream margarine and 1 cup sugar together until fluffy. Add eggs and vanilla and beat well. Blend in sour cream. Add dry ingredients. Spread half of batter in greased and floured 9-by-9-by-2-inch pan or bundt pan. Sprinkle raisins and a mixture of nuts, 1/2 cup sugar, and cinnamon in pan. Pour remaining batter on top. Bake at 350 degrees about 40 minutes. Frost with Creamy Lemon Icing.

Creamy Lemon Icing

1/2 cup shortening (part butter recommended)
4 tablespoons all-purpose flour
1/4 teaspoon salt
1/2 cup lemon juice
3 cups confectioners sugar, sifted
1/2 teaspoon vanilla extract
1 teaspoon grated lemon rind

Melt shortening in saucepan. Remove from heat; blend in flour and salt. Stir lemon juice in slowly. Bring to boil, stirring constantly. Boil 1 minute; remove from heat. Stir in confectioners sugar and vanilla, blending until thick enough to spread. [Place pan in ice water while stirring to set the icing.]

Ice Cream Cake

1 10-ounce angel food cake
1 11-ounce can Mandarin oranges, drained
1 8-ounce can crushed pineapple, drained
1 10-ounce package frozen strawberries, thawed
1/2 gallon vanilla ice cream, almost melted
1 box strawberry Jell-O
1 box lime Jell-O
1 box orange Jell-O

Break cake into bite-size pieces and place on three separate sheets of waxed paper. Sprinkle each mound of cake with one box of dry gelatin dessert. Layer ingredients in tube pan as follows:
- strawberries
- cake with strawberry Jell-O
- 1/3 of ice cream
- crushed pineapple
- cake with lime Jell-O
- 1/3 of ice cream
- Mandarin oranges
- cake with orange Jell-O
- 1/3 of ice cream

Cover pan with plastic wrap and freeze. Unmold and serve. Prepare cake the day before it is served.

Poppy Seed Cake

1 cup shortening
3 cups sugar
3 cups all-purpose flour, sifted
1 cup buttermilk
6 eggs, separated
1 teaspoon salt
1/2 teaspoon baking soda
1 tablespoon poppy seed

Cream sugar and shortening. Add egg yolks one at a time. Sift together flour, salt, and soda; add alternately with milk. Beat egg whites and fold into mixture. Stir in poppy seed. Pour mixture into bundt pan. Bake at 325 degrees for 1 hour and 15 minutes, or until done, when a toothpick inserted near the edge of the pan comes out clean.

Apple Nut Cake

great with coffee for informal morning get-togethers

1 cup English walnuts
2 cups sugar
2 cups all-purpose flour
2 teaspoon cinnamon
1 teaspoon nutmeg
1/2 teaspoon cloves
1 teaspoon salt
2 teaspoons baking soda
2 eggs
1/2 cup vegetable oil
1-1/2 teaspoons vanilla extract
1 20-ounce can apple pie filling

Mix dry ingredients together. Add eggs, oil, pie filling, and vanilla; blend thoroughly. Bake in greased 12-by-9-by-2-inch oblong pan. Bake at 350 degrees for 1 hour. Sprinkle with confectioners sugar.

Poppy Seed Cake #2

1 yellow Duncan Hines Deluxe cake mix
1 package instant French vanilla pudding
1 teaspoon almond extract
1/2 cup vegetable oil
4 eggs
1 cup milk
4 tablespoons poppy seeds

Mix all ingredients together and pour into greased and floured bundt pan. Bake 45 minutes at 350 degrees. Cool 10 minutes in pan, then invert on cake rack. Sprinkle confectioners sugar on top.

Glazed French Applesauce Cake

1 package Duncan Hines yellow cake mix
1 package French vanilla instant pudding
4 eggs
1/3 cup vegetable oil
1/3 cup sour cream
1 cup applesauce
1 cup finely chopped raisins
1/2 teaspoon cinnamon
1/4 teaspoon nutmeg
1 cup chopped pecans

Combine cake mix and instant pudding in a mixing bowl. Add eggs one at a time, beating at medium speed. Add remaining ingredients and blend well. Pour into greased and floured bundt pan. Bake at 350 for 55 minutes. Cool in pan 15 minutes.

GLAZE

1 tablespoon milk
1 cup confectioners sugar

Mix together well and spread on cooled cake.

Aunt Lill's Mt. Fuji Japanese Fruit Cake

1 cup butter
2 cups sugar
4 eggs, separated
3 cups all-purpose flour
1 tablespoon baking powder
1 cup milk
1 teaspoon cloves
1 teaspoon allspice
1 teaspoon cinnamon
1 pound raisins, chopped
1 cup chopped nuts
Maraschino cherries and whole nuts for garnish

Cream butter and sugar until light and fluffy. Add egg yolks, one at a time, beating well after each addition. Mix flour and baking powder together and add alternately with milk. Beat egg whites until stiff and fold into batter. Divide batter into two parts. Put one part in refrigerator until later. To the remaining batter fold in the spices and raisins. Pour into three greased and floured 9-inch pans. Bake at 350 degrees for 20 minutes. (The layers are very thin, so they don't take long to bake.) Remove the second part of the batter from the refrigerator. Fold in the chopped nuts. Bake in three layers as directed above. Cover each layer with Lemon Coconut Filling.

Lemon Coconut Filling

juice and grated rind from 4 lemons
juice and grated meat from 1 fresh coconut, separated
2 cups sugar
1 stick butter
2 cups hot water
1 cup water, room temperature
6 tablespoons cornstarch

Combine all ingredients except coconut and cook on low heat until bubbly and thickened. Cool till you can comfortably touch the side of the saucepan.

In putting the cake together, alternate spice layers and nutty layers. Spread each layer with filling and coconut. Garnish top with cherries and whole nuts. No additional frosting is needed for this cake.

Apricot Nectar Cake

1 box Duncan Hines Lemon Supreme cake mix
3/4 cup vegetable oil
1/2 cup sugar
4 eggs
1 cup apricot nectar

Mix oil, sugar, and cake mix together. Beat in eggs, one at a time. Blend in apricot nectar. Bake in greased and floured bundt pan at 325 degrees for 1 hour.

Banana Cake

2-1/2 cups all-purpose flour, sifted
1-2/3 cups sugar
3/4 cup evaporated milk
1/3 cup butter
1/3 cup shortening
1 teaspoon salt
3-1/2 teaspoons baking powder
1/2 cup milk
3 eggs
1 teaspoon vanilla extract
3 bananas, sliced

Cream sugar, butter, and shortening. Combine flour, baking powder, and salt and add alternately with milk, eggs, and vanilla to creamed mixture. Beat 2 minutes at medium speed. Bake in three greased and floured 9-inch layer pans at 375 degrees for 25 minutes. Cover each layer with sliced bananas and spread with Lady Baltimore Frosting (Seven-Minute White Icing). Stack layers, covering all with icing.

[NOTE: I use this recipe for coconut cake, leaving off the bananas and adding grated fresh coconut to the icing.]

Lady Baltimore Frosting
(Seven-Minute White Icing)

2 egg whites
1-1/2 cups sugar
1/4 teaspoon cream of tartar
1/3 cup water
1 teaspoon vanilla extract

In top pan of double boiler, combine the egg whites, sugar, cream of tartar, and water. Cook over medium heat, beating the mixture with rotary beater, about 7 minutes or until the frosting is stiff enough to spread. Remove pan from boiling water and stir in vanilla.

Lemon Cake

1 package Duncan Hines yellow cake mix
1 package lemon Jell-O
3/4 cup vegetable oil
3/4 cup water
4 eggs

Combine cake mix, Jell-O, oil, and water; mix well. Beat in eggs, one at a time. Bake in greased and floured bundt pan for 1 hour 15 minutes at 375 degrees.

GLAZE

2 cups confectioners sugar
juice of 2 lemons
grated rind of 1 lemon
2 teaspoons lemon extract

Blend confectioners sugar and lemon juice. Stir in extract and lemon rind.

When cake is done, remove from oven and stab with a knife. Pour glaze over cake and return to oven for 5 minutes.

COOKIES

Benne Cookies

3/4 cup butter
1-1/2 cups brown sugar
2 eggs
1/4 teaspoon baking powder
1-1/4 cups all-purpose flour
1/2 cup benne seeds, toasted
1 teaspoon vanilla extract

Cream butter and sugar together. Blend in other ingredients. Drop by teaspoon onto greased cookie sheet. Allow enough space for cookies to spread. Bake at 325 degrees for 30 minutes.

Bonnie Doone Plantation Thanksgiving Cookies

2 cups all-purpose flour
3/4 cup granulated sugar
3/4 cup brown sugar
1 teaspoon baking powder
1 teaspoon vanilla extract
1 egg
2-1/2 cups rolled oats
1 cup raisins
2 cups cranberries, pitted and mashed slightly
1 cup chocolate chips
1 cup melted butter
1 cup chopped walnuts

Combine all ingredients. Batter will be slightly stiff. Drop by teaspoon onto greased cookie sheet. Bake at 375 degrees for 10-12 minutes.

Peanut Butter Cookies

2-2/3 cups sifted all-purpose flour
2 teaspoons baking soda
1 teaspoon salt
1 cup butter, softened
2/3 cup creamy peanut butter
1 cup granulated sugar (plus extra for rolling cookies in)
1 cup brown sugar
2 eggs
2 teaspoons vanilla extract
5 dozen chocolate kisses

Sift flour, baking soda, and salt together; set aside. In large bowl beat butter and peanut butter with electric mixer at medium speed until well blended. Add sugar and beat until light and fluffy. Add eggs and vanilla; beat until smooth. Stir in flour mixture. Using a level tablespoon measure, shape batter into 5 dozen balls. Roll each in granulated sugar. Place 2 inches apart on ungreased cookie sheet. Bake at 350 degrees for 8 minutes. Remove from oven and press a chocolate kiss in the top of each. Bake 2 minutes longer. Remove cookies to rack and let cool.

Party Chocolate Cookies

2 egg whites
1 cup confectioners sugar
1/3 cup crumbled saltine crackers
1 12-ounce package chocolate chips, melted

Beat egg whites until stiff and add sugar. Fold in saltines and chocolate. Drop by teaspoon on greased cookie sheet. Bake at 350 degrees for 13 minutes. [Cookies will not be smooth on top.]

Persimmon Cookies

1 cup sugar
1/4 cup shortening
1 egg
1 cup persimmon pulp
2 cups all-purpose flour
1 teaspoon baking soda
1 teaspoon salt
1/2 teaspoon cinnamon
1/3 teaspoon cloves
1/4 teaspoon nutmeg
1 cup raisins
1 cup chopped nuts

Cream sugar, shortening, and egg. Add persimmon pulp. Sift together flour, soda, salt, cinnamon, cloves, and nutmeg. Add to persimmon mixture. Fold in raisins and nuts. Drop by teaspoon onto greased cookie sheet. Bake at 375 degrees for about 15 minutes.

Savannah

Gen. James Edward Oglethorpe, a member of English parliament, was a guiding force behind the colony of Georgia. When he agreed to lead a party of settlers to the New World, he was in the prime of his life and stood tall and handsome. Oglethorpe was an English gentleman in the truest sense.

In 1732, Oglethorpe and 114 pilgrims set sail from England on the *Anne*, arriving in Charles Town on January 13, 1733. There, Oglethorpe asked Gov. Robert Johnson for help in finding a site for his group. The people of Charles Town were delighted to be of assistance, because the new settlers would live on land between them and the Spaniards, who had settled Florida.

From Charles Town, Oglethorpe sailed to Beaufort, South Carolina, where he met with Col. William Bull, a civil engineer. Oglethorpe and Bull left the new settlers in Beaufort while they sailed down the coast to survey the land. The general wasn't happy with the first site Bull pointed out, but when he saw the second, he knew he had arrived at the settlers' new home. The spot was beautiful. A bluff rose some forty feet above the river and offered nearly a mile of frontage on the water. There was ample room for a large settlement. Oglethorpe and Bull returned to Beaufort with the good news.

On February 1, 1733, the colonists landed on the western end of the bluff and from there made an easy ascent to the tableland. They erected tents of pine, cedar, and evergreen oak branches.

Oglethorpe and Bull soon marked out a village square, adjoining streets, and lots for homes. On February 10, the general recorded that the first house was already under construction. The new town was named Savannah.

From the time of these first settlers to the present, Savannah has been a place rich in history and folklore. One of the best ways to explore this wonderful city is through its legends.

The Ghost
of Bonaventure

Bonaventure Cemetery has always been one of the loveliest spots on the east coast. People have visited the site for more than two hundred years to view its beauty.

This tract of land in the Thunderbolt section of Savannah, adjacent to the Wilmington River (part of the Intracoastal Waterway), was settled around 1760 by an English colonel named John Mulryne. Mulryne's plantation was named *Buono Ventura*, Italian for "good fortune." The place proved to be true to its name. The large brick mansion was noted even in England for its great beauty. Terraced gardens extended from the house to the river.

When Mary Mulryne, daughter of Col. John Mulryne, married Josiah Tattnall of Charleston, the wedding was a marked event in the annals of Savannah's society. In honor of the union, Colonel Mulryne ordered several avenues of live oaks planted on the grounds in a pattern to form the letters M and T. (Those oaks still stand in Bonaventure Cemetery today.) Mary and Josiah had two sons, John and Josiah, Jr. Their portraits were hung in the Tattnall home near that of their grandfather, Col. John Mulryne.

When the Revolutionary War broke out, loyalties in Savannah were greatly divided. In 1778, Josiah Tattnall, choosing to remain faithful to the beliefs of his father-in-law, refused to fight against England. He was thereafter shunned by the local patriots. And, Buono Ventura, although the rightful property of Colonel Mulryne, was confiscated. The colonel was angered at the seizing of his estate and strongly objected, shouting, "The papers. The papers. They prove my ownership." Fearing for their safety and seeing no other recourse, the Mulrynes and Tattnalls set sail for England.

Of Mary and Josiah's sons, John sided with his father and became a lieutenant in the King's Rangers, while Josiah, Jr., only twelve years old, protested earnestly against leaving his birthplace.

Josiah, Jr., returned to America at the age of eighteen and reclaimed Bonaventure. He distinguished himself by becoming a member of the Georgia congress and a governor of the state. He died in 1804 at the age of thirty-eight in the West Indies where he had gone seeking to recover his health. During his life, he had frequently expressed the desire to be buried beneath the oaks at Bonaventure, where he had played as a child. According to his wishes, he was laid to rest beside his beloved wife who was already buried there.

Josiah, Jr., left an orphaned son, Josiah, III. Custody fell to the boy's grandfather, Josiah Tattnall, who was still living in England. The grandfather had the young boy brought to England to be educated. Six years later, Josiah, III, returned to America and joined the navy.

Like his forbears, Josiah, III, struggled with his dual allegiance to the United States and England. On one occasion, he deserted the American navy to come to the aid of the British fleet, which was fighting in Chinese waters, an act that drew international attention. When he was reprimanded for breaching America's neutrality in the event, Josiah, III, simply replied, "Blood is thicker than water." His remark played well in England, and actually helped bring about the first positive feelings between the two countries since the War of 1812. The distinguished military career of Josiah Tattnall, III, lasted to the time of the Civil War, when he served as a commodore for the Confederates.

In 1845, during the time Josiah, III, owned Buono Ventura, Mrs. E. F. Ellett of Savannah visited the plantation. By that time the property was generally known as Buonaventure. Mrs. Ellett recorded the following narrative, which was published in the *Columbian Lady's and Gentleman's Magazine* of 1846:

> It was toward the end of April 184— that I visited Buonaventure, in company with a party of friends, most of them strangers to the locality. An individual from Savannah, who kindly acompanied us as guide, was extremely communicative in regard to the different per-

sons who had been owners of the ground. . . .

"Was there anything remarkable about it [the house]?"

"Why, nothing that one could speak of, at least in its outward appearance. It was a gloomy looking building enough, with old-fashioned windows, and the broken down wall you see yonder, surrounding it. . . . To speak plainly, it had the reputation of being haunted."

All laughed at the idea of a haunted house in Georgia at this day.

"You may laugh if you will but it was true nevertheless. I know many who would not have passed a night there for any reward. And why should not ghosts appear nowadays, I wonder, as well as in old times, when there is occasion for them?" . . .

Of course we all inquired concerning the particulars. . . .

"As I told you, rumor said there were appearances in the house that could not be accounted for. The old story was revived about the transfer of the inheritance. There was a law-suit concerning it in my grandfather's time; but the person whose father had held the property could not make good his claim, by reason of his failing to produce the documents that secured his title. So his opponent gained the cause; though almost every one thought his claim an unjust one." . . .

"A hard lot, if unjustly deprived of his property."

"Precisely; and that brings me to the wonderful part of my story; which proves that Providence does, indeed, watch over human affairs. I shall tell it, notwithstanding you may ridicule what I say."

". . . Pray let us hear the rest."

"My father," continued our guide, "has often told this to me; and I know him to be incapable of any departure from truth. He was not married at the time it happened, and was a stranger in this part of the country. He was hunting, in February, in the woods with a party of friends. It was after dark before they were ready to return, and you know what a tedious ride it is now, because of the sand, between here and Savannah. The road was then difficult to find for one unaccustomed to the forest, and my father proposed asking the hospitality of the gentleman who lived in the house I have been describing for a night's lodging. The others refused, alleging as a reason the rumors they had heard. My father was as incredulous as yourselves, and with a laugh protested that he feared neither ghosts nor devils enough to take a long ride through the woods, on an uncertain road. . . .

"The others were not of his mind; and so my father begged an introduction to the gentleman of the house, from one of the hunters, and they all rode up to the gate. The proprietor was an open-hearted man, of courteous and obliging disposition, as almost all our Southern landholders are. He received the whole party with a cordial welcome, invited them to remain all night, and insisted at least on their staying to supper. His excellent wine caused the guests to be very communicative, and in the course of conversation, all that had passed between my father and the others came out. The host smiled as he heard it; but some thought his smile a forced one. At all events, when my father asked leave to stay till next morning, and his companions begged that he might be put into the haunted chamber if there was one, he promised to satisfy them to the extent of his power. The whole party made an engagement to meet next day at dinner in the hotel then standing at the corner of Monument Square, in Savannah, that they might hear all that had passed. The host accepted an invitation to join them. Then, as it was late, the hunters had their horses brought to the gate, and departed. My father remained alone and conversed with his new acquaintance, who seemed a man of much intelligence and information, till bed-time. . . .

"As the host conducted my father to his chamber he observed with a smile, that he was sorry he had no haunted room for his reception, which might afford him an adventure, and a subject for their dinner's discussion. 'But I will give you,' he said, 'the old library apartment, that was formerly occupied by my father, both as study and bed-room. There are some curious volumes in it; they will give you plenty of stories of apparitions, if you choose to consult them. . . .'

"It was a large, old-fashioned room into which my father was shown; with several shelves, on which were old leather-bound volumes, some in folio. He examined several that excited his curiosity, and found them valuable relics of past ages—illuminated manuscripts, ornamented with rare and curious paintings. The owner of the house had a fine taste in such things. The room was also hung with several portraits of members of the family. The paintings were fine, though much soiled by smoke and dust: and had in the candlelight quite a life-like appearance. It was late when, after examining them, for he had a great fondness for pictures, my father retired to rest.

"He was awakened from a profound slumber by the clock striking. It struck three. He was surprised to find it so late. The moon was shining faintly in at the windows, and fell in a line of silver on the polished floor. Every object in the room was visible, though not directly in the light, the long table, with the candlesticks, the books, the massive oaken chairs, and a marble urn that stood in the corner.

"In a few moments, to the surprise of my father, the clock struck one; it had struck three quarters before. At the same time he thought he heard a rustling in the apartment, as of some one moving behind the curtains of his bed. He partly rose from the pillow, and looked around. Gradually, as vision returns to one who has been dreaming, he became conscious of seeing a figure seated in a large leathern chair, just beneath one of the portraits. It was that of a man, dressed in regimentals, as the portrait had been, and with a face so exactly similar, that my father involuntarily glanced at the picture. What was his astonishment to see the frame empty!

"The other portrait frames that hung around the room were empty also! At the same time he perceived other figures moving about, or seated in the chairs. One was that of an old lady in a stiff brocade, that rustled as she moved; another a younger female, with a bridal veil upon her head; another a middle-aged man, with a roll in his hand. Between these moved a number of other figures, less distinctly seen, their faces being hid in the shadow, and their forms, as it were, blended together. There was no noise of footsteps; but my father could hear voices whispering, and even distinguish some of the words they uttered. He thought he heard one lady, who had seated herself near the bed, say to another, 'Are we to have no music, or dancing, any more?'

"The military-looking man seemed the superior among them. Almost every one looked to him with an expression of deference; but he appeared regardless of them, and his face exhibited both concern and melancholy. He walked to and fro, my father said, with unequal steps, now stopping short, now pushing forward through the crowd, as if intent on something the rest knew nothing about. Once he came close to the bed-side, and my father saw that his features were noble and expressive, though the countenance was overcast with sadness.

"Suddenly he went up to the middle-aged man, who was standing motionless in the middle of the room, and attempted to take the roll from his hand, saying something, of which my father could only distinguish the words, 'My children,' and 'The papers,' spoken rapidly and in seeming agitation.

"So great was the interest my father felt in this scene, that he forgot his fear of supernatural appearances, and watched with intense curiosity the face of the military man. This personage, after taking a few turns, in apparent perplexity, through the apartment, again went up to the middle aged man, and said in a low voice, but distinctly, 'Be just—be just! yield up what is not your own! Let not the innocent suffer.'

"The other shook his head slowly; the military man turned his face so that the faint light fell upon it; and my father saw that it was distorted and dark with contending passions. The face of no living human being could have expressed so much, with such wild and terrific energy. The sight was a fearful one; my father closed his eyes shudderingly; and the next moment the whole scene faded away. The outlines of the figures first became tremulous and indistinct; then they seemed to melt into one another; and at length all was dark, for the moon went down behind the hills. A strange drowsiness, or rather exhaustion, overcame my father and he fell into a deep slumber, from which he did not wake till late in the morning, at the entrance of a servant to inquire his commands. My father's first glance was at the portraits. They were all in their frames as he had seen them the preceding evening; and the picture of the military man hung directly opposite him.

"The host was particular in his inquiries as to how he had rested; but my father, for many reasons of his own, chose to say nothing of what he had seen. He expressed, however, some curiosity about the portraits, which the gentleman of the house was very willing to gratify. Some of them were ancestors of his own; and the man in military dress he described as having been an officer in the old war, to whom the estate had originally belonged. His right had been disrupted, after his death, by another branch of the family, who succeeded in establishing their claim and obtaining possession after the tedious lawsuit I have mentioned.

"My father said nothing to all this; nor did he relate to the company he met at dinner, the least of what had occurred. There seemed, he said, a sort of sacredness in this confidence of the dead; besides, how could he have convinced them it was not all a dream, or a delusion of his imagination? . . .

"My father might have thought so, *himself*—but for a singular occurrence. Many years later, some workmen employed in digging a well—there, you may see where it has been filled up—near the house, found a half mouldered piece of parchment, on which the writing was nearly defaced. It was one of the documents so long lost; and though insufficient, without others that could not be found, to establish the right of those who had been deprived of the property, yet it proved such writings to have been once in existence. But the wronged heirs were no longer to be found: the estate had been dismembered and was greatly diminished in value; and nothing was ever done with the recovered parchment. It was sufficient, however, to convince my father that what he had seen was no dream. . . .

"Since then," concluded the narrator, "to the day of his death, he could never look on a portrait . . . without a sort of horror."

There was no use in attempting to shake the belief of our friend in his marvelous tale; so no further attempt was made. We only thanked him for his narration.

In 1850, Capt. Peter Wiltberger, owner of the Pulaski Hotel, purchased Bonaventure and turned it into a cemetery. It was called the Evergreen Cemetery of Bonaventure until July 1907, when the property passed into the ownership of the city of Savannah and was placed under the jurisdiction of the Park and Tree Commission. Since then, it has been known as Bonaventure Cemetery.

The remains of Josiah Tattnall, III, lie in Section E of the cemetery, along with those of his parents and several Tattnall children who died in infancy.

The Man Who Bought Himself Three Times

Dimmock Charlton was born in Africa, in a country called Kissee, on a great river "away up on the fresh water." In 1858 he was, he believed, about fifty-eight years old, and he remembered vividly the first twelve years of his life, when he was called Tallen. A wild, untutored, and happy boy, he had never heard of Christian men or nations. But then a war broke out between his own and a neighboring tribe, and his people were conquered. Tallen was among the prisoners who were captured and driven to the coast to be sold to slavers.

Compared to the hundreds already huddled together at the seashore awaiting their fate, the number of prisoners on the journey from Kissee was scant. The natives were led toward anchored ships. Other tribes were equally as wretched as the tribe from Kissee as they were herded onboard a Spanish vessel. The voyage that followed offered three weeks of horror. The little boy from the great "fresh water" of central Africa, who had never heard of civilization or been taught to believe in any other God than Fetish (an object believed to have magical power), took his first step toward the knowledge of Christian life. Tallen came to believe that his new God helped him endure the horrors of the "Middle Passage." He listened to the groans of the dying and suffered himself the agonies of thirst and suffocation. He saw his fellow passengers, who had fallen victim to death, taken on deck to be thrown into the sea. At the end of the three weeks, the Spanish ship was captured by a British cruiser, and the vessel—and what was left of her human cargo—was taken to England.

On the arrival in England a pleasant prospect seemed to open before Tallen. On the dispersion of the Africans, it fell to his lot to be put onboard the British brig *Peacock* as a cabin boy. That vessel soon set sail. Tallen would, for the rest of his life, consider himself a British subject.

On the Atlantic, the *Peacock* was confronted by the American schooner *Hornet*, and in the memorable naval battles that followed, Tallen was again taken prisoner. He was given the name John Bull and carried to America.

John Bull became the charge of Lt. William Henry Harrison (later, president of the United States) and was taken to Savannah. In that city he was left with Judge Charlton, until ordered to Washington, to be disposed of with other *Peacock* prisoners. Judge Charlton proposed to Lieutenant Harrison that he leave the boy with him to be brought up, but the lieutenant declined, stating that as prisoner, John Bull was not within his control. Two months passed before Judge Charlton was asked to deliver his charge. Word was sent to Washington that John Bull had died of the fever.

Bull was, of course, very much alive. Judge Charlton called together his servants, and announced to them it was his pleasure that hereafter the boy should no longer be known as John Bull, but by his own surname—Charlton. John Bull that day became Dimmock Charlton.

Judge Charlton, a man of high standing and respectability, and a lawyer of some eminence, committed a despicable crime. After giving the boy his very own name, he sold him the following day to John P. Setz, a Frenchman. Dimmock protested that he was nobody's slave, but a free man. Setz, on the other hand, condescending to reason on the subject, asserted that the judge owed him some money for a bill of clothes. Setz was a tailor, and the boy was given to him in lieu of payment. An appeal was made by Dimmock to the judge, but the judge denied that he had sold him. Dimmock soon learned, however, that the judge was indebted to Setz for his body servant Isaac, and the judge had sent Dimmock in his place.

Dimmock was taken by Setz to Augusta, on the advice of the judge, and about a year later he was sold to a Mr. Dubois, a steamboat captain. Dimmock lived with Dubois two years, and was then sold successively to Captain Davison and William Robinson of Savannah.

During these years Dimmock began to realize that he would be more successful in his bid for freedom if he found some other avenue of escape than protesting against slavery. Dimmock was an industrious man and in the course of time he made enough money in his business as a stevedore to purchase his freedom from Robinson for the sum of $800. Dimmock had no sooner paid the money than he was sent to jail and kept there for sale until a new buyer was found for him. The slave code explicitly stated that a slave could possess nothing, and all that he had or could earn belonged to his master. Therefore, the $800 Dimmock hoped would purchase his freedom had by law already belonged to Robinson.

James Kerr, of Savannah, was Dimmock's next owner. Kerr expressed a great deal of indignation when told by Dimmock of the manner in which money had been taken of him by his former master. Encouraged by this sympathy, Dimmock again commenced the accumulation of funds for a second purchase of his freedom. Kerr agreed to accept as ransom the sum Dimmock had originally paid to Robinson. At length, Dimmock put into Kerr's hand $800.

During this time with Kerr, Dimmock had become a husband and father. A Mr. Pratt owned his wife and children, and he consented to sell them at a moderate price to anyone who would hold them for Dimmock until he could redeem them. Dimmock, who had paid Kerr's asking price, interceded with his master to purchase his wife and two children, with the understanding that the purchase be credited to Dimmock's account.

Kerr consented and the purchase was made after Dimmock put into his hand an additional $1,500, which he had accumulated from his business. The sum Dimmock expected Pratt to ask was $2,000, and the balance of $500 he promised Kerr to make good. Kerr accepted the trust, and went to Pratt, making the purchase for $600.

When Dimmock discovered the purchase price, he was appalled at the breach of trust and confronted Kerr for an accounting. Dimmock demanded that Kerr return to him $900, but Kerr laughingly responded that it was safe in the bank. He gave Dimmock a written obligation for it. This obligation Dimmock put into his trunk. On an occasion when Dimmock was absent from home, his trunk was broken open and the paper stolen. That the paper alone was the object of the thief was evident from the fact that the fifty dollars, which lay beside it, was untouched.

For many years following, Dimmock lived contentedly with Kerr, believing his freedom and that of his family was secure, and that they could not be again sold or separated from each other. The monetary transaction between the man and his master was, Dimmock felt certain, entirely in accordance with the usual way of business between whites and blacks. Therefore, he took no special precaution against further knavery, nor was he aware that such precaution was possible.

But the time arrived when Kerr again broke his word. He sold Dimmock to one man and Dimmock's wife to another. Their children were scattered among various owners. Dimmock fell into deep despair. He had always believed himself to be a British subject and wrongfully held in slavery. Hudson, the man who had purchased him from Kerr also believed it, and probably considering that he may have made an unsafe investment, sent Dimmock to a trader to be sold again.

A liquor dealer purchased him. But on learning his story, put him again on the market. Dimmock was bought this time by Benjamin Garmon, who permitted him to purchase himself and leave Savannah a free man. Dimmock had bought himself for the third time.

He began to search for his grandchild, named Ellen, the only member of his family whom he believed he could emancipate. He wanted to free her and put her beyond the reach of accident or hostile design. He believed he knew where she was living, and his greatest desire was to secure her liberty and happiness. He told his story to the morning *Times*, and it appeared in print. When Dimmock read the article, it occurred to him that he had possibly made a dreadful mistake. The person who had possession of the child would, he feared, when thus warned of the presence of the grandfather, be careful to put her beyond his reach. Dimmock's conjecture was well founded, as the child was living with two Kerr women, sisters of his former master. After reading the article in the *Times*, they left town.

The Misses Kerr were located and questioned about their past movements, their present residence, and their plans for the future. Their intentions, they said, were good. Their only wish was to secure the happiness of the little girl, and to this end they had instituted a subscription for her adoption.

As Dimmock had no money for legal fees and no one seemed inclined to help him, he boarded a ship for England. Somewhere in Georgia he had a wife, children, and at least one grandchild. Although he had bought himself three times, he had no means with which to buy his family. He desired to spend his last years in England. After all, the little boy from the great "fresh water" of central Africa still considered himself a British subject.

Wilmington Island
Oyster Roast

The oyster roast has been a favorite way of serving oysters since the Indians lived in Georgia. The roast is one of the state's most fashionable winter "sports" and every stranger to the region must needs be entertained in this alfresco manner during the season. Evidence of this fact lies in the many pieces of broken grill and banks of oyster shells found all along the seashore—evidence that has obviously taken hundreds of years to build.

There are many ways of preparing oysters—on the half shell, in a chowder, stewed, and fried. But because of the informality of the occasion, the ease of preparation, and the appetizing results, there is still no more popular way of cooking the oyster and of entertaining large groups of people than the oyster roast. These affairs are usually held during the months whose names end with the letter "r"—when oysters are plump, plentiful, and delicious.

A little over a hundred years ago, on a visit to Savannah, a midwesterner was asked if he had ever been to an oyster roast. He replied that he had not but would very much like to, as he had never heard of one. He was curious as to how an oyster might be roasted.

The next day his host set about making plans with a group of friends for one of those delightful gatherings. The following Wednesday was decided on for the day of the event. Since one of the men owned a plantation on Wilmington Island, he invited the group to have the outing there.

Wednesday dawned clear and cold, an ideal December day for the roast. There was much excitement as the men in overcoats and mufflers started out at ten o'clock that morning. They wanted to be on the island early, so the visitor could watch every step in the preparation of the oysters.

Earlier that morning, Uncle Ed, an old servant, and his son Mose, armed with oyster tongs, had gone out on the river in a bateau (a double-ended, flat-bottom rowboat). Oystering was usually done at low tide when the choice oysters could be seen more readily.

Uncle Ed's son Silas had stayed behind to look after preparations for the cooking. Long pieces of metal were stretched on bricks and logs a few feet from the ground. Wood was gathered for the fires, and long tables placed about the grounds.

While the men were busy with the oysters, Aunt Jane and fifteen-year-old Sarah had prepared a savory sauce for dipping. This sauce was made of about one pound of melted butter, four quarts of tomato sauce, Worcestershire sauce, one cup of lemon juice, some good dashes of hot pepper sauce, salt, and black pepper. Bowls of the savory sauce, crackers, pickles of all kinds, and plain tomato sauce were placed on each table.

The visitor was full of wonder as he and the other guests arrived. He had assumed that an oven was necessary to roast anything. He walked over to Uncle Ed and inquired, "Where are the oysters cooked?"

"We just pours 'em out on dat hot tin, kivers 'em up wid wet crocus sacks so as to steam, an in 'bout fifteen minutes you see 'em pop open. Dey's just right den, and you got to eat 'em right now. Dey ain't no good cold."

After a few minutes he saw Aunt Jane and Sarah bent over a big iron pot from which a savory steam was rising. Strolling over, he asked, "What have you in the big pot, Aunt Jane?"

"Mister, dat sumpn' you ain't never had befo' an I knows it. Dat gonna be shrimp pilau [pe-laf]."

"How do you make it?"

"Well, I ain't got it done yit, but it a-comin'. I tell you fur as I bin' an you kin stay here and watch de res' fur yo' sef.

"I cut me up 'bout one pound of good bacon in little pieces an fry dat down to git all de fat. Den I put me in six big onions, four bell peppers, an a little stalk of celery—all done chop up fine.

"When dat git kinda brown lak, I dumps in six jars of tomatoes all mashed up. All dat gonna stew down 'bout ten minutes."

The visitor noticed a bag of rice and some raw shrimp. "Is that the way the shrimp look when they are caught, Aunt Jane?"

"No, suh. When dey come out de river dey in a shell wid heads, feets, an beards. I pull de head off, an squeeze de body through the shell. Cose I washes off de sand an grit too."

"Do you put in the rice and shrimp at the same time?"

"No. De rice come next. I washes it an washes it agin fo I puts it in. I gonna use twelve cups of rice, an when dis all cook 'bout fifteen minutes, I just kinda folds in my shrimps, make de fire low as I kin an let 'er cook 'bout one hour. After everything in de pot, I sprinkle in slow 'bout a big han'ful of salt, an some pepper—fo it git good done. Ef dat ain't 'nough, I adds some more. You don' never stir pilau while it cookin'. You must raise 'em up an down wid a long kitchen fork."

Sarah asked her mother if they were going to have hoe cake.

"Child, you know I'se gonna have hoe cake. I wouldn't give dese white folks no seafood widout a hoe cake."

Turning to the man, she asked, "Have you ever et a hoe cake?"

"No," he said dubiously.

"Well, I done mix up some cornmeal dis mornin' an set it aside. I mix as much meal as I want wid bilin' hot water jest so I kin pat it out. I adds my salt an leave it set a w'ile. Jest fo it time to eat, I puts it on the greased griddle in cakes 'bout half an inch thick an browns both sides. We always has hoe cake wid our seafood an vegetable dinners down here what we lives."

The man asked her how in the world it had ever come to be called hoe cake, and she told him, "Well, a long time ago befo' dere was any stoves, folks used to bake it on the iron end of a hoe set up before de fire. Dat why it called hoe cake."

By this time everyone was hungry and the steaming hot oysters were taken up in shovels and poured on the tables ready to be eaten. All had gathered around, each one armed with an oyster knife to open the oysters and with a fork to take them out. Sometimes when the oysters are hard to pry open with the knife, the shell has to be chipped away. To do this, the handle of the knife or a piece of shell is used. Aunt Jane brought out the pilau and hoe cake in plates, and cups of steaming hot coffee were plentiful.

The visitor soon found himself lifting the piping hot oysters out of their shells with as much ease as if he had a lifetime of practice. The plump morsel, dipped in the spicy sauce and swallowed in one juicy mouthful, was a treat, he agreed, for the most jaded appetite. To his astonishment he put away several dozen oysters without even realizing it.

Late in the afternoon when the visitors were ready to return to Savannah, it was agreed that nothing could surpass an oyster roast for good things to eat and genuine fun. Aunt Jane was so elated when complimented on everything she had cooked that she tried to tell the visitor of all the good southern dishes she could prepare.

"Nex time you come I gonna make you some crab stew an some oyster chowder like only me knows how to make. I also gonna make you some rice spider bread. I makes dat out of flour, rice, an eggs, an cooks it in a spider."

"What in the world do you mean, Aunt Jane, by cooking it in a spider?"

She laughed and said, "I knowed dat would git you. A spider is a old time skillet but it got straight sides an stan on three legs. Dat why it called a spider. De hot ashes can be raked under it so de bread git hot through an through."

Double Bad Luck Day

Today Pin Point is in one of the most beautiful sections of Savannah, but in the 1930s it was about nine miles southeast of the city. Small wooden cabins were spruced up by whitewashing, and most of them were nearly hidden by overhanging foliage or Spanish moss that draped the oak trees. Each cabin had a front porch, under which a dog or two lazily snoozed. Chickens pecked in the sandy yards. Any sunny spot was planted in vegetables.

Also at Pin Point was a church, and the residents of that area attended regularly, although they believed perfectly in conjure, spells, hexes, hags, and other superstitions that had come to Georgia many years earlier.

Most of the men and women worked at the crab cannery, and some of the women were employed as domestic servants in Savannah. For diversion, they hung out at the pavilion, near the crab cannery on Moon River.

The prime residential area of Pin Point today is still on the Moon River. The Intracoastal Waterway, bearing white yachts that travel to Florida for the winter and Cape Cod for the summer, sparkles in the distance. Some residences, houses and mobile homes, are ill-kept, with muddy driveways. Scattered debris and goats speckle the yards. The old crab cannery is still there, along with a huge mound of crab shells. The upscale residential neighborhoods are only a mile away. Beautifully landscaped Bethesda Boys Home is nearby. And the activity brought on by big city Savannah is all around. A new sign welcomes you to Pin Point, and it designates the area as the former home of Supreme Court Justice Clarence Thomas.

In 1932, Pin Point was, for the most part, a quiet community, but occasionally some scandal concerning a resident brought on a frenzy. Like the time a Pin Pointer ventured as far away as the Ogeechee River, about ten miles distant, and was consumed by an alligator. All that was left of him, they say, was "the ham," which was buried amidst boisterous and passionate expressions of grief.

On another occasion as adults and swarms of children were gathered together eating crabs—biting into the soft part of the body shell or cracking a claw with strong white teeth—they learned about the bottle that had been burrowed in Lewis McIver's mattress. Lewis had been ill, but after the bottle was discovered and removed from his mattress, he recovered quickly. "Somebody had something 'gainst him and plant it there," someone uttered. "And Lewis ain't have no more pain since it was took out."

Pin Point attained its highest measure of fame in 1932 for the Bo-Cat murder.

Limerick "Bo-Cat" De Lancy killed his wife Catherine and dropped her corpse into the deep waters near Hell's Gate. Discovery of the murder drew considerably more attention when it was noted that Bo-Cat had killed Catherine on a "Friday the thirteenth," a particularly dangerous day on which to commit a murder. Margaret Snead, remembered the events well.

> Wy, duh night Cat'run De Lanzy was kill, she spen' it in town wid me. Aftuh dat night I didn' see huh no mo'. People frum duh Pint come inquirin' 'bout huh but nobody seem tuh know nutt'n 'bout huh weahbouts. 'Bout two week latuh, a pahty ub wite mens wuz out huntin' an' come 'cross duh body at Raccoon Keys—a ilun 'yond Hell's Gate. Mus' be mone twenny mile frum duh Pint. I don' see as how nobody could carry a puhson dat fuh jis tuh mudduh 'em. Anyway, duh body come tuh be brung tuh duh city, an' at duh unduhtakuh's office people go in to see kin day 'dentify it. Dis a hawd t'ing tuh do. Huh been in duh watuh fuh days 'fo' a high tide wash duh cawpse tuh sho'. Duh body caught 'tween two logs weah duh buzzuds wuk on it.
>
> I 'membuh a great big cawn Cat'run suffuh wid but couldn' nebbuh git rid ub. So I wen' in an' had a look at duh foot, an' sho 'nough deah wuz dat cawn, jis like it use duh be wen huh wuz libe.
>
> Huh ole husbun, Limbrick De Lanzy, awready 'rested, an' he git sen' up fuh life. It be May duh thuhteent dat ole Limbrick carry Cat'run off down duh ribbuh an' muhduh huh. A double bad luck day—a Fridee an' duh thuhteent.

Margaret was asked if the body was buried at Pin Point.

> Yeah, it wuz. But we didn' hab no settin' up cuz duh body wuz too fuh gone. Dat wuz sad. Ebbybody lub Cat'run. Fuh huh tuh die an' be bury widout a settin' up, widout lettin' anybody view duh face aw lay day han's on it, wuz sho a pity.

According to Margaret, everybody was at the funeral. They came from miles around to pay their last respects to a poor wife murdered by a husband on Friday the thirteenth.

> Duh body wuz brung frum duh unduhtakuh's pahluh straight tuh Sweet Fiel' ub Eden Chu'ch at duh Pint. Chu'ch so crowded you couldn' hawdly see duh coffin up in front. We sing hymns, an' den wen duh singin' die out, you could heah jis a little hummin' heah 'en dere. Somebody stood up an' said 'Cat'run De Lanzy wuz a sistuh ub duh Lawd!' Somebody else say, 'She sho wuz. She wuz a chile ub Jesus an' she walk in duh way ub righteousness.'

Each person in the congregation got up and gave testimony to Catherine's goodness. Some people cried and screamed as they told the mourners, at least one hundred in all, what a fine woman Catherine had been.

> Den duh remains wuz took tuh duh cemetery heah at duh chu'ch an' wuz buried. Duh whole time we singin' hymns an' sway tuh duh soun' ub duh music. Ebbybody t'rew a hand'ful ub dut in duh grabe an' wen duh grabe digguhs fix duh moun', we put some ub Cat'run's t'ing' on duh top. Deah wuz a little flower vase wid duh bottom knock out, an' a lamp chimney, an' some perfumery bottles, an' duh pitchuh she made ice watuh in jis 'fo' Bo-Cat took her off. Den duh preachuh 'nounce duh fun'ral suhmon wuz tuh be preach at duh annu'l memorial wen day pray fuh ebbybody who die duhin' duh yeah. Den we all gone home.

Margaret was asked why Limerick De Lancy was called Bo-Cat.

> Deah a' no significunse tuh dat. I hab a fr'en' dat ebbybody call Fridee, but huh name is Lula. I hab a

son name of May Bud simply 'cause he born in May. One ub my brothuhs wuz call Baby Head 'cause he born wid a big head. No. I don' pay no nebbuhmine to names, but I do pay 'tention to bad luck dates. Look at po' Cat'run De Lanzy, deprive ub all duh proppuh t'ing' dat come 'fo' burial, 'cause it wuz a double bad luck day. Fokes at duh Pint say dat spirit nebbuh will res' in duh grabe.

The fact that Catherine had been murdered on Friday the thirteenth spun into significance, and in time inspired a ballad. Attributed to no single author, it seems to have evolved over a period of time.

On the thirteenth of May
You could hear ole Bo Cat say,
"Git my deed an' policy,
Turn it in the ashes way."
Then ole Catherine she begin to inquire.
Didn't know ole Bo Cat had them In the fire.
It a shame how Bo Cat done he wife.
Put her in the boat,
They begin to float,
They float to the Raccoon Keys,
He knock her on the knees.
Catherine holler, "Na-Nan-Na."
It a shame how Bo Cat done he wife.
He knock her in the breast
And the oar done the rest.
It a shame how Bo Cat done he wife.
He knock her in the back
And the oar miss and crack.
It a shame how Bo Cat done he wife.
When Bo Cat went back home
He meet her daughter all alone.
And daughter say, "Bo Cat, Bo Cat,
Where my mama is?"
Bo Cat turn right out his head
And he throw her 'cross the bed.
It a shame how Bo Cat done he wife.
They got Bo Cat in jail
'Bout to hang him by the rail.
It a shame how Bo Cat done he wife.

Black Ankle

Once upon a time, in a village near Savannah, lived many families whose ancestors had come from England. The people had no concept of being poor or rich, and their values were true and steady.

The village was situated on an isolated strip of country bordered on one side by the Ogeechee River and along the other sides by heavily wooded marsh and tracts of pine forest through which no passable roads had been built. It was a solitary spot, so beautiful its wild landscape would have been an Eden for the nature painter. The village was nearly inaccessible so that its inhabitants were cut off from the outside world and lived as a virtual backwoods community. In Black Ankle, as the village was called, the England of another day survived.

The name Black Ankle was descriptive of the village dwellers. Strangers attached the appellation when they came upon the colony and found men, women, and children going barefoot through the Low Country mud, their ankles continuously coated with black ooze. The settlement was divided into three sections: South Newington, Bethel, and Spring Hill, all good English names. But to outsiders it would be Black Ankle long after new roads and modern progress crossed its borders.

It happened one day in 1925 that Black Ankle attracted attention from the outside world. Some fishermen and a party of pleasure seekers returned to Savannah with tales of a wild man who took shots at them from behind trees along a certain section of the Ogeechee River. It was dangerous, people came to believe, for a stranger to venture into that unknown territory. Communities on the fringe of the district reported that a strange hostile tribe of white people lived there, that members of the group rarely emerged from the isolated spot, and that the colony was apparently bent on retaining its seclusion.

A hunter was once lost for several hours in the jungle-like labyrinth of the Black Ankle forest. While seeking a way out of the woods, he heard the cracking of twigs and the rustling of leaves as though somebody was following him. Several times he thought he discerned a whisper or a hiss. But in all his hours of search, trying to get his bearings, he saw no human soul.

Government agents eventually made their way into the district. In an automobile and armed with a pistol, they pushed inward along an old broken, weedy path that only a solitary wagon had traveled at long intervals. They crossed two ditches bridged with ancient logs and discovered Black Ankle as it had been for a century. Houses were one-room log huts like those built by the early English settlers. There was no school, no government, no modern touch to indicate that the twentieth century had transformed civilization. Cooking utensils were nonexistent save for frying pans and gallon tin cans. Electricity and gas were unknown. The marvels of the outside world were incredible myths to these folk. They lived much as their ancestors had lived when they first closed themselves off many years before.

To the county officials they presented a hostile front. The women and children scurried like frightened mice out of sight, taking refuge in the huts. They peeked fearfully, but with great curiosity, through the chinks in the boards. The men stood close-mouthed, unfriendly, and suspicious, their fingers ready on the triggers of sawed-off shotguns. Before one of the strangers could speak, a shrill feminine encouragement to battle issued venomously from behind a closed door.

"Git 'em, paw! Git 'em!"

Half Moon Lake, surrounded by overhanging trees, formed a crescent of shadowy water on the west side of the land. In the years when the old Ogeechee Canal flowed past Black Ankle, providing a means of communication with Savannah, this man-made lake was a part of the dam that controlled the overflow of the Ogeechee tides. When the canal fell into disuse, it was allowed to dry up, isolating the people of Black Ankle, but the lake remained and became in time as natural a part of the scene as the river that gave it life. The surface of the lake was covered with wild hyacinths of India, off-spring of a single bulb imported to the region years earlier. The purple blossoms floated alongside the delicate, fragrant petals of water lilies. Birds and tiny animals found sanctuary in the deep entangled forests of cypress and other hardwood trees that grew, crowded, down to the water's edge. It was a paradise for any naturalist. From Half Moon Lake the woods extended into the canal bed where Ogeechee lime trees flaunted their bright red fruit. Throughout the district was cassena, in its rarer yellow variety as well as its red-berried species, and iris and dogwood grew in profusion. Many tropical plants, including the white-flowered stewartia, a member of the dogwood family, also thrived. Along the eastern border the land elevated to a ridge of white sandy soil in which only tiny scrub oak and pine grew.

Who were these people who called this lovely wilderness home? Outsiders wanted to know. How had they changed since the dried-up Ogeechee Canal shut them away from the rest of the world? The answers could be found in their habits, customs, and traditions, which were definitely Old English. Their names, which were as Anglo Saxon as their coloring, also provided clues. Families had lived on the same land for generations and great clans had grown up. The people held no deeds; they knew only that long ago their forefathers had laid claim to the land and it was theirs. When they were asked how long they had been there, they replied, "Allus been hyar."

The next few years following the opening of the district to outside influence, there was little change in the psychology of the Black Ankle inhabitants. They still looked with hostility on strangers, accepting only those individuals who had become known to them, like the tried and true county workers. They resisted change, seeking desperately to hold onto the remarkable preservation of their ancestral customs. When a rural mail route was offered to them, they refused to sign papers because the receipt of letters was unknown among them.

With the development of good roads in the area, they began to see automobiles. When a strange vehicle drew too near their homes, however, they would disappear in an instant.

So untrusting were these people of the outside world, even medical attention was slow to be accepted. Nurses at first had the utmost difficulty persuading parents to allow their children to be given treatment for hookworm, which was a common ailment among the youngsters. As for vaccination and diphtheria serum, these were absolutely out of the question. The nurses were compelled to resort to force; they had to hunt for many a child in the bushes behind the houses. One little girl's vaccination caused her arm to swell, and when the nurse made her next house call, she found the father grimly waiting with a newly-oiled gun.

"If'n yuh don't take yore spell outen that child's arm," he shouted, "I'll blast yore brains out, yuh witch."

In this isolated community of sixty to sixty-five families, intermarriage worked inevitable evils. The percentage of low mentality among both old and young was distressing. One young girl told the county agent that her father, resenting her marriage to a "foreigner," had divorced her.

"But how can he divorce you?" the agent asked.

"He jist done it. He said he wa'n't a-going to have no furriner in his family."

The agent discovered that the "foreigner" was a native of Brunswick, less than a hundred miles away.

The inbreeding had preserved the English features—the blonde hair, the blue and gray eyes. Brown eyes and dark hair were the exception.

The oldest and largest clan was the Carter family, and two other powerful groups were the Douglas and Wise clans. Other surnames were Richards, Horning, Burgess, Bashlor, and Hargroves. Girls responded to old-fashioned names like Aletha, Geneva, Eunice, Vivian, Alverina, Theolia, Ursula, and Vandela. Boys were named John, Thomas, Leander, Cecil, and Paul. New names rarely crept into the region and mothers often made up appellations for their new children.

Black Ankle fishermen stretched their shad nets out along the river bank to dry. One day a handsome young man from one of the older families ran amuck. With a razor-sharp carving knife, he made his way up and down the river bank slashing every net in sight, including his own. Brandishing his knife and shooting—with all his neighbors as audience—he destroyed the patient labor of months, for Black Ankle fishermen wove their own nets by hand. The young man was in such a state, it took three policemen from nearby Bloomingdale to bring him under control. As they were taking him away, one of the officers quietly asked an onlooker what had caused the trouble.

"Oh, he jest got provoked," was the answer.

In the entire district there was only one brick house. It was a rust-colored dwelling whose principal feature was a fine old hardwood floor of planks, each a foot wide. Beside the front door grew a japonica bush, so old its tangled branches had attained the thickness of tree limbs. There was only one two-story structure in Black Ankle, the Douglas homestead. Originally a low, long house, it had been embellished during the prosperous days of Prohibition with an upper floor. The remaining houses were one-room huts enlarged to meet a family's needs by adding small lean-tos. The head of each family served as carpenter. Each clan built around the old homestead, but often two or three miles separated the groups from one another. These huts, though small and humble, were characterized by scrubbed pine floors.

The people of Black Ankle did not work at trades. There was no necessity for labor of this sort in a region where fishing, hunting, and trapping produced ample returns, and fruits grew wild at back doors. For generations the people had been fisherfolk and hunters, selling the catch of both stream and woods to small rural communities up and down the river. Bootlegging also furnished financial return. Liquor stills were plentiful in the hidden recesses of the forest. The stranger who came upon one accidentally did not soon forget the astonishment and shock of being confronted by a flint-eyed ancient with a sawed-off shotgun who ordered him in gentle tones to "git outen these hyar parts."

Sometimes at dusk when the music of the forest life began its night-long orchestration, a woman's voice crooned a lullaby. The words were perhaps her own, perhaps her grandmother's, but the melody was one heard often in the past beside an English cradle.

These simple folk hummed the airs of "Annie Laurie" and "Bobby Shaftoe," but until the coming of the outer world they had never heard a blues song nor the intricate rhythm of sophisticated jazz.

Their dances too were corruptions of the English country dances of a bygone era. They hopped, skipped, and ran—backward, forward, and in circles—patting hands, pointing toes, swinging partners to an old rollicking repetitious tune. The old grandfather of a clan frisked through the steps with a greater accuracy than his progeny. However, the dancers were rarely caught unaware. If they had a suspicion that they were being "spied on," they instantly stiffened, resentful, and walked off with stoical faces.

Superstition was a dominant factor in the life of Black Ankle. The scanty planting done in the community was undertaken only when the moon was a narrow arc above the marsh. Even adults ran in mortal terror if they thought they saw a ghost, and belief in witches and hags was strong. To sew on Sunday was to stick the devil every time the needle penetrated the material. It was believed that babies could be marked somehow if the expectant mothers were frightened or otherwise disturbed.

The remnants of religious practice had remained Episcopalian, though the influx of society in later years influenced a change in favor of the Holy Roller sect. At both Bethel and Spring Hill there were small wooden buildings that for generations had served as churches. As the Carter clan was established all around the Spring Hill Church, they claimed it as theirs through inheritance. Other folk attended, but the strong males of the Carter tribe were self-appointed elders who governed the church activities with a grim determination. Black Ankle people had services perhaps once a month when an itinerant preacher arrived. Leaving fish hooks, guns, and stills, they entered the house of the Lord for an hour of worship. Personal cleanliness was a characteristic of Black Ankle residents and, except for their dusty bare feet, their bodies were clean and shining.

Religion degenerated in the district and eventually even Christmas and Easter passed unobserved. Strangely enough, though, strict ideas on the holiness of Sunday and the sacredness of the church building held sway. The time came when a community center was housed in the old Spring Hill Church. A woman tried to put a cookstove in the building and seven brothers, elders of Spring Hill, administered an indignant and wrathful verbal chastisement.

The lack of religious training, however, had not affected the kindly attitude of Black Ankle dwellers toward one another. A man would not let his neighbor go hungry, and often he would spend an entire morning assisting a friend to build a shed. A woman would take in any unfortunate child and treat it as her own. They were extremely mindful of each other, yet how differently they behaved toward strangers. A young botany student, after hours in the woods, came upon a Black Ankle house before which stood a woman and a group of barefoot, tallow-headed children. When he asked for some water, he was given a long, level stare, after which the whole gathering stalked into the house and closed the door. He was told later that because he wore khaki trousers he had been perhaps mistaken for a "revenoor."

The district recognized no central authority; it was ruled by clan law, and the matriarchal system was most favored. Each of the larger clans vested high authority in its eldest female member. These hardy and tyrannical old ladies demanded absolute respect of their numerous relatives.

Mrs. Douglas, eighty-five years old and weighing two hundred pounds, was a prominent personality in the region. She was one of the few adult members of the village who did not shy at visitors. One morning when a friendly woman, who was tolerated because she was a government worker, stopped at the Douglas home and asked to be directed to the residence of a certain Tod Horning, Mrs. Douglas graciously replied that she would get her boy to act as guide.

"He's somewhar round about," she remarked. Not seeing him in the yard, she opened her mouth and emitted a bellow so loud and shrill it shook the air. An instant "halloo" from some distance away was the response. Then followed a conversation in the same penetrating key.

"Sheddy?"

"Yes, ma'am, Mama."

"Whar be yuh?"

"Down tew th' creek."

"What be yuh a-doin?"

"A-fishin'."

"Well, I'm a-comin'. Stay thar."

Explaining that the Horning place lay beyond the creek, the old woman led the way behind the house and down a path. The agent picked her way cautiously, but Mrs. Douglas's bare feet trod unconcernedly on wet grass, twigs, and rough earth.

"Sheddy's a good boy," she said. "Most young men is gal crazy but Sheddy ain't never been one to be a-studyin' of gals."

A turn in the path brought them to the shallow creek formed by the backwash of the swamp waters. "Thar he is now," the old woman pointed out.

Sitting on a log with a fishline in the water was an old man of more than sixty seasons. His tanned countenance was wrinkled. His gray beard reached down to his chest. But he was Mrs. Douglas's *boy*. He eyed the newcomer warily but did not shift the position of his long, lanky body. His mother, however, tore the line from his hand.

"Look at yuh, Sheddy. Look at yuh. Yore face is as dirty as a cooter's, an' this hyar lady a-wantin' yuh tew guide her over tew Tod Horning's. Ain't yuh 'shamed! Go wash yore face this minit."

"Aw, but mama, I washed hit this mornin'. Why should I wash hit again jest tew go over tew Tod's? He ain't nothin'."

"Git a move on thar an' don't yuh dare tew sass me."

"Yes, ma'am, mama."

With trousers rolled above mud-coated feet, the old man shuffled off around the curve in the path. His mother, her ample sunbonnet figure outlined against the great, dark loom of the woods, stood and watched him go. A drift of thick smoke from her pipe curled upward and disappeared.

When communication with Savannah was finally established, a group of two or three Black Ankle residents would sometimes ride to town with the county agent, or proudly come in a car of their own purchase, for a day of shopping. Wearing outlandish garments, they leisurely strolled about, staring and pointing. Modern civilization was to them incredible. Accustomed to rude implements and only the barest necessities, they stood before display windows amazed. Few new gadgets, however, found their way into Black Ankle homes. Ingrained distrust of the unfamiliar prevented expenditure on "sech silliness."

On one of these visits to town the agent took three of the ladies to lunch at an old southern tearoom. The guests clucked delighted astonishment at everything they saw. They were particularly impressed with the iced tea and remarked on its lovely tinkle, its color, its flavor.

"That's somethin' to remember forever an' ever always," said one woman. "Iced tea. Whoever would a-thought of hit in this world?"

Cattle in Black Ankle were allowed to run wild. They were rarely milked as their chief use was supplying beef now and then when the appetite balked at fish and small game. Unlike other communities of the Georgia Low Country, whose cooks invariably seasoned vegetables with bacon, the Black Ankle inhabitants used only salt, a culinary practice that prevailed in rural England. The women did not sit at the table with the men. They first served their "lords," then they and the children dined together.

The principal foods were bream, shad, rabbit, corn, rice, beans, scuppernongs, and wild pears. The submarginal soil was good for little except the dwarf trees for which the Pine Barren Road was named. Marmalade was made from the Ogeechee lime. That bitter lime was known in England in the twelfth century, and it is believed to be a native of southern China or Burma. But on the coast of Georgia, the bitter fruit simply meant marmalade, and it had too harsh and acrid a taste to be consumed straight from the tree. All homes in Black Ankle had lime trees growing amidst the shrubbery. As the trees did not get very tall and their green leaves were waxy, they made a perfect ornamental shrub. Today one can only dream of the heady fragrance that must have wafted on the soft breezes from the lime tree blossoms that resembled tiny stars.

To make marmalade, the fruit was first weighed. Every part of it was used in the process that followed. The limes were cut in half and the juice squeezed through a sieve. Peels were set aside. Seeds were put in a bowl of water, which after a time jelled. Loaf sugar was added to the juice, and when the seed jelly had formed, that was added to the sugar and juice mixture. The next step was to boil the peels, changing the water five or six times, until the bitterness had been sufficiently extracted and the peels were tender. Several peels were set aside and the remainder pounded with a mortar until soft. The pounded peel mass was added to the juice and sugar mixture, which was cooked until thick, having been stirred frequently. The peel that had been set aside was cut in pieces and added for extra texture and flavor.

Some of the old-time residents of the Black Ankle community still live in the area today. But for the most part, people like Mrs. Douglas and her son Sheddy have long since passed away.

The area that once supported the village of Black Ankle is now a part of the beautiful countryside surrounding Savannah. The Ogeechee Canal has been cleaned, and one can see the old locks and the huge overhanging trees. Bethel Church is nearby, and many Black Ankle residents are buried in the cemetery across Little Neck Road from the church.

Madam Truth

"Everything that happens is caused by conjure or magic," said a woman of Sandfly. "They just don't leave nothin' to God."

Although the residents of Sandfly strongly believed in hexes, spells, spirits, hags, and the like, they went to church regularly, were baptized, composed and sang spirituals with red-hot excitement, and prayed long, fervent prayers. That's the way it was at Sandfly, on the Isle of Hope.

The Isle of Hope has existed for many years, and today remains one of Savannah's showplaces. The ruins of the manor house at Wormsloe Plantation, which boasts the longest avenue of oaks in the southeast, are there. Noble Jones, who came to Georgia on the *Anne* with James Edward Oglethorpe, the Englishman who founded and served as first governor of the colony of Georgia, owned the plantation and built the manor. The waterfront property on the Isle of Hope is among the most picturesque in the country.

Madam Truth lived at Sandfly, a settlement on this stunning island. She kept her house pristine and was always neatly dressed. On first meeting, Madam Truth appeared an ordinary woman. But those on the island knew another side. The people of the Isle of Hope visited her in the same manner the people of Beaufort went to Dr. Buzzard for treatment. If they wanted an early prophecy regarding the outcome of a business affair or the direction a courtship was taking, they pushed aside their fears of Madam Truth and went to her for answers. When she conducted a seance, as she often did to get her answers, her persona changed. Her voice became lower-pitched; her hands moved involuntarily this way and that; and her eyes rolled back in her head. When Madam Truth entered her trance, there was no telling what would happen next, and her followers were terrified.

Madam Truth was a deeply religious person and she insisted

that, as part of her treatment and diagnosis, her followers attend the Holy Sanctified Church of Sandfly in order to be baptized. Sermons in that church were a delicious throng of sensations. The undertone of hand clapping and drumming of feet swelled and died with the ebb and flow of the preacher's rhetoric. Moses and Job were the most popular subjects of sermons, and occasionally there was a lesson on the prodigal son. The prayers that were uttered and songs that were sung had been generations in the making and were native to the Isle of Hope. There were frequent responses of "Amen." As primitive as the services were, they were things of true beauty. The various parts of the service fitted together harmoniously in a way that made the whole a sort of sacred chant.

The lines of baptismal candidates on the way to the river was long. Always attired in white, they marched to the tempo of the song they were singing. "I'm going down to the river of Jor-a-dan," they sang.

One day a man came to Madam Truth and told her he was near death.

"A spell been put on yuh?" she asked.

"I ain't had no sleep in more'n a week or so," he said. He went on to explain that he believed he had been conjured. Someone had put a set of teeth in his house. Since that time, all night long his house shook, and a great voice demanded, "Bring back us teeth!"

"Did you bring 'um back?" Madam Truth wanted to know.

The man took the teeth from a pocket and slapped them down on a table in front of her. "Give 'um back!" he shouted.

Madam Truth got up and closed her curtains. She sat down at the table and went into a trance, her hands moving in circles just over the set of teeth.

"I be gettin' deep knowledge," she said as her eyes rolled back in her head. "The sperit be showin' me everything."

The man went to a sofa and sat down. He was pale and weak, and the airless, dark room didn't help. He said nothing.

Finally Madam Truth stopped the seance. She got up and opened the curtains. The man looked at her with an expression of uncertainty.

"The sperits say to warn you not to eat any fish or cabbage," she said. "They say to give you that message. And they say for you to go to church on a regular schedule and be baptized."

The man got up and put his hands in his pockets. "I sho do that all right."

"After the sun gone down on your house, you won't shake no more," Madam Truth promised. "The voice will leave you alone. It won't bodder you no more."

"What 'bout the teeth?" the man asked.

Madam Truth put the teeth in a deep pocket of her apron and again told the man he would lose no more sleep. She insisted that he go home and not forget to attend divine services on Sunday.

Two months later Madam Truth saw the man. He had gained weight, was energetic, and appeared to be healthy. She asked him how he was. "Have you eaten any fish or cabbage?"

"No. I jes sleeps like a log," he said, smiling. "Can't hardly get my work done. All day long I wants to hit the hay."

"I've seen you in church," she said. "I'm glad your health has been restored to you."

Madam Truth didn't explain the rudiments of the treatment. She had always held that when a person believed a hex had been put on him or her, that person sometimes heard voices, suffered a loss of good health, and believed perfectly that the hex would continue until death. However, if that person visited a witch doctor and had a hex removed by someone who was stronger than the person who had applied the hex, the spell would go away, and the patient would recover robust health. It was all in the mind of the patient.

Mrs. Habersham's Terrapin Stew

Ward McAllister (1827–1895) lived a proper life, divided between the cities of New York, Newport, and Savannah, where he was born. He must have inherited his desire to hobnob with the very rich, because his great-grandfather on his mother's side, the Rev. Gabriel Marion, was also the grandfather of Revolutionary War hero Gen. Francis Marion. McAllister's father was a Savannah lawyer who served for years as mayor of the city.

Newport, Rhode Island, was then considered a southern colony and it was the fashion to send one's family there for the summer. If, for some reason, the McAllisters did not go to Newport for the summer, the humid "sickly" months were spent at the family's cottage at Springfield.

Springfield was near New Ebenezer, which was near Savannah, and area Salzburg transplants were the predominant residents. From Salzburg, Austria, had come a colony of Lutherans seeking a new country and freedom of worship. They arrived on March 12, 1734, aboard the *Purlsburg*. They settled on the banks of the Savannah River and named their settlement New Ebenezer. Many people wondered how such large families were sustained on such small farms. The secret was that everybody worked. There you found the most economical housewives and the most frugal husbands in Georgia. It was said that any New Ebenezer wife could take a large sweet potato, serve it to the family in a half dozen different forms, and feed "Fido," "Old Brindle," and the pigs on the residue.

Ward McAllister was a strong, confident young man and made his presence known at an early age. In 1842, when he was 15, McAllister read the Declaration of Independence on the fourth of July from the pulpit of Jerusalem Lutheran Church at New Ebenezer.

About this same time, he and his brother, who were members of the Debating Society, opposed one another publicly on the question, "Which is the stronger passion, love or ambition?" Ward advocated love. The good men hearing the debate decided in Ward's favor.

McAllister's brother followed in his father's footsteps and studied law, setting up a practice in San Francisco.

Ward remained in New Ebenezer, becoming a man-about-town, and was frequently invited to dine at the home of his relatives, the fashionable and wealthy Telfairs, and their friends. It was at Mrs. Fred Habersham's table that he discovered her famous terrapin stew, a taste for which he would carry with him the rest of his life. Mrs. Habersham's terrapin stew was to Savannah what Lady Baltimore cake and benne cookies were to Charleston. Long before Ward McAllister became a prince among epicures, and an overnight sensation for the turning of a phrase, he yearned for another plate of Mrs. Habersham's terrapin stew "with plenty of eggs—a dish for the gods." Thus he began the search for the recipe. Getting an accurate accounting of ingredients and cooking time, however, wasn't as uncomplicated as it may seem. Mrs. Habersham's kitchen, of course, had several cooks, and getting directions from them was rather like trying to write down the music to the spirituals they sang. They cooked as they sang and played musical instruments "by ear."

"How long do you cook your okra?" a cook was asked.

"I puts it on when I puts on the rice."

"And how long do you cook the rice?" the cook was asked.

"Till dinner's ready."

Finally, after myriad requests, Mrs. Habersham conducted a cooking school at her home in Savannah, and all the young society matrons gathered once a week, pencil in hand, and wrote down the words of wisdom that fell from her lips, while she demonstrated cooking as she talked. It was likely from one of these young society matrons that Ward McAllister obtained the recipe.

McAllister moved to New York and resided with his father's cousin, a woman whom he called "Aunt." The house was a fashionable one on Tenth Street. Food for the table came from the woman's

Georgia plantations. Turkeys arrived in barrels, having been bled, but not picked or cleaned of their insides. Wild turkeys from Georgia were considered a delicacy in New York, and McAllister reminisced, "It was turkey hot and turkey cold, turkey tender, and turkey tough, until at grace one would exclaim, 'I thank ye, Lord, we've had enough.'"

It was while McAllister was a resident at this house that he began to be invited to the city's high society balls. The first one was at the home of Mrs. John C. Stevens in her residence on College Place. A company of soldiers had been called in to drill on the waxed floors to perfect them for dancing. It wasn't long before McAllister was invited to the Schermerhorns' house at the corner of Great Jones Street and Lafayette Place. All the guests were asked to appear in costume of the period of Louis XV. The lace and diamonds on the women astonished even the members of society.

McAllister felt that his Aunt would endow him with all her worldly goods, which were plenty, but she chose over him the Presbyterian Church and the Georgia Historical Society. So, after her death, he returned to Savannah with the intention of studying law. That study, however, did not take up all his time, and he attended Savannah balls and recited poetry to beautiful southern ladies. His brother notified him that he was making money hand-over-fist in San Francisco. Ward left Savannah for that city, his father with him. He had passed the Georgia bar, and his lawyer friends ridiculed him for entertaining the thought of going to San Francisco. Worse still, in the opinion of the legal community, his father, who had been appointed a Superior Court judge, was also *turning his back* on Savannah. The idea of these men pulling up stakes and going to the outpost of civilization seemed absurd.

Nevertheless, the Savannah home was sold, the law office closed, and on May 13, 1850, the pair left for California. In two years the father had amassed such a large fortune he moved to Europe.

McAllister built a house for himself and ordered his furniture from Paris. His bed quilt, a Chinese floss silk shawl, set him back $250. "Such dinners as I then gave, I have never seen surpassed anywhere," he said. When McAllister's father was told about the establishment of his fine house, his response was, "Yes. Ward keeps everything but the Ten Commandments."

Ward returned to New York and again was invited to the Schermerhorn house. This time he had a plan: Caroline Webster Schermerhorn was to become the most famous lady in the history of society.

Marriage placed Caroline in the position to lead New York society. In 1853 she had married William Backhouse Astor, Jr., a grandson of John Jacob Astor. Over the ten years that followed the marriage, they produced a quartet of daughters. It wasn't until 1872 that Ward McAllister would become Mrs. Astor's spokesman and turn her name into a household word in the world at large.

McAllister was a gentleman and perfectly suited to act as Mrs. Astor's collaborator. His Georgia wife, Sarah Taintor Gibbons, was so meek and retiring most people soon forgot her existence. He took her with him, however, when he went to Europe to refine his knowledge of food, wine, and the social niceties. There, he developed an acquaintance with Queen Victoria's chef and wangled invitations to fortnightly balls given by the Grand Duke of Tuscany at the Pitti Palace. In addition to all his newly acquired knowledge of dining, he had Mrs. Habersham's recipe for terrapin stew.

McAllister encouraged Mrs. Astor to trim her guest lists to include only the three Bs: birth, background, and breeding. Additionally, he and Mrs. Astor stipulated the proper time for dinner, the correct table service, and the correct fare. From there, Ward McAllister and Caroline Astor created the society that would forevermore be known as "The Four Hundred." Through it all, his favorite dish remained Mrs. Habersham's terrapin stew.

MRS. HABERSHAM'S TERRAPIN STEW

3 large terrapin, boiled and picked
6 hard boiled eggs
3 heaping tablespoons flour
1/2 teaspoon grated nutmeg
1 onion
1/2 pound best butter
rind of 1 lemon

1 pint sweet cream
1 tumbler good wine or 1/2 pint sherry
red pepper and salt to taste
1 tablespoon Worcestershire sauce

Rub yolks of eggs and butter and flour together. Put on jelly or stock to cook, and as soon as it boils, add egg mixture, also lemon and nutmeg. Then put in terrapin eggs and meat, and last of all, the cream and wine. Be careful not to let curdle or burn. Add chopped white of eggs. Always have enough hot milk to thin out if it is too thick.

Prepare terrapin before making the soup. Cut off heads, dip in boiling water for a short time, and carefully pull off outer skin from feet, and all that will come off the back. With a sharp hatchet cut open the terrapin, and take out the eggs, and put aside in cold water. Throw away entrails and gall bags, saving the livers, which are very much liked. Leave all the legs on the back and put on to boil. Put into about three pints of water, with salt and onion, and let simmer and steam (not boil) about forty-five minutes. When tender, take meat from back and remove bones. Cook meat a little more if not tender enough. Cut up meat—across the grain to prevent stringing—and set stock aside to jell. Then forget it for a few hours (if you can) and when the party is imminent, proceed as above.

NOTE:

Terrapin is an edible North American freshwater turtle.

Savannah

The Boastful Planter

Three of the brightest spirits and most noble Englishmen known to Ward McAllister, world traveler and society leader from Savannah, were Lord Frederick Cavendish, the Honorable Evelyn Ashley, and G. W. des Voeux, who later became governor of Hong Kong. McAllister believed each of them to be the epitome of English gentility.

Through his own life, McAllister offered up an original definition of that rarest of rare birds—the English gentleman. From the battlefield at Agincourt to the playing fields of Eton, he had consistently proven himself to be one of the world's wonders. An English gentleman, it is known, was not defined by what he did but by what he was. Chaucer's "parfit, gentil knight," as an example, was a chap whose position was determined not by law nor popular vote—nor by class. He was in a class by himself.

While the three aforementioned English gentlemen were visiting McAllister in New York, the host decided to take them down to Savannah and treat them to a taste of the Old South. It just so happened at that time, a friend of McAllister offered the use of his home for a month, fully staffed with servants. The foursome left New York immediately, as a cold snap had descended and snow flurries were in the air. When the guests arrived in balmy Savannah, McAllister forsook no detail to make the Englishmen comfortable, including the provision of an enormous cedar washtub and warmed towels, in the savoir vivre of England's royal houses.

McAllister was eager to show the Englishmen the fine homes in the Savannah squares as well as those in the surrounding countryside. He desired also to display the English knowledge of polite society to the people of Savannah. Most Savannahians were of English descent, and they worshipped English nobility.

As McAllister had hoped, word of the party's arrival reached

Savannah's hosts and hostesses, and the foursome from New York had only to choose at which tables they would be seated during their visit.

A Savannah picnic was an Old South institution, and McAllister lined one up immediately. The group left the city in a river steamer, and after a voyage of about an hour on the familiar Atlantic, the party reached Daufuskie Island, off the coast of South Carolina near Hilton Head. A charming residence situated amidst five acres of roses provided the setting. Huge baskets containing their dinner, a full table service, and Madeira were carried to a place under the trees. A cloth was laid on the ground, and fine porcelain china and crystal wine glasses were arranged on it. McAllister had been a connoisseur of wine from an early age.

In Savannah and Charleston, from 1800 to the time of the Civil War, afternoon wine parties were the custom. Guests were invited to arrive at 5:00 PM for Madeira. (This was after the 3:00 PM dinner, which was the principal meal in the townhouses as well as on the plantations.) Mahogany tables were polished to a fine shine for the gathering, and each place setting was laid with four glasses, olives, parched ground nuts, and finger bowls. There were never fewer than half a dozen bottles of Madeira for each table.

Madeira was ordered by the pipe for upscale Savannah households. In one single order, it is reported, five hundred pipes of Madeira were shipped to Savannah by the firm of Newton, Gordon, Murdock & Scott, the major supplier to Low Country planters. The wines were known as *extra* Madeiras. All men of "the quality" ordered at least one or two pipes each year.

After the Daufuskie Island feast, those attending the picnic danced in the warm, moist sea breeze. They twirled, dipped, and waltzed on a platform that had been set up in the rose garden. As night approached, they sashayed back to the steamer and returned to Savannah by moonlight.

The next Savannah tradition McAllister introduced to his English friends was the sport of game hunting, southern plantation style. McAllister sent a note to a plantation baron, strongly hinting at his desire for an invitation to take his guests on a deer hunt. The invi-

tation was received by return post. The very next morning at first
light, McAllister and his friends set out for the plantation. It was
late that same day when they arrived. The hunt was scheduled to
begin the following morning. At the appointed time, the guests were
awakened by the tooting of horns and were soon on their merry
way. The deer hunt proved so successful, McAllister asked his guests
to hunt quail the next day, in a different section of the countryside.

Early the following morning, with a guide to accompany them
and bird dogs to assist them, the men started out on horseback in
pursuit of quail. From field to field, hour after hour, the men went
until they began to grow very hungry. McAllister thought of the hot
biscuits that were served on country tables, and he asked the guide
if there was a house within a mile or two where they could get a
biscuit. There was only one house, according to the guide. It was
on a very large tract of land, but they would get nothing there.

"But we are starving," McAllister pressed. "Do you not believe
the cook at that house would spare a biscuit or two for some weary
hunters?"

"Not at that house," the guide explained. "You couldn't get a
crust of bread there."

McAllister knew the area pretty well, as it was within a dozen
miles of Savannah. But he didn't know who lived in this particular
house. "To whom does the house belong?"

The guide gave the name.

"What are you saying?" McAllister asked, dumbfounded. "Are
you telling me that is the house of Mr. Jones, the man who owns
such a lovely home at Newport, Rhode Island?"

Suddenly McAllister was eager to point out to his visitors the
features of the Jones "cottage" in Newport. After his marriage, Ward
McAllister had bought a farm on Narragansett Bay and was acquainted with all the socialites who had mansions in that city.

McAllister explained that the Jones's Newport house had been
designed by Richard Upjohn, a Welshman and designer of Trinity
Church on lower Broadway in New York City. The house, he said,
had gables trimmed with carved pinnacles and serpentine barge-
boards, and the eaves were bordered with pendant trefoils. A long

porch graced the east side. Inside the house, a gold-plated French porcelain dinner service for twenty-four was used in the dining room. The library was filled with leather-bound books. And the cellar had a large inventory of the finest wines.

"That's the man," the guide said. "It's one and the same."

"I know him well," McAllister said. "I visit Newport each year. Many times Mr. Jones has asked me to visit his Savannah plantation. He lives like a prince. I saw him not long ago at Ochre Point [the site of the magnificent Vanderbilt home, The Breakers], and Mr. Jones turned up his nose at everything."

McAllister went on to say that Jones had commented that Newporters didn't know how to live. Why, down in Savannah, he had said, he owned so much silver the city vaults were stuffed with it. Jones was from a very distinguished family. His ancestor had accompanied Gen. James Edward Oglethorpe to Georgia.

McAllister insisted that the guide lead them to the home. He could hardly wait to show such a fine plantation manor house to his friends.

The four hungry men and the guide reached the plantation. They were a ragtag crew as they made their way down the avenue of oaks toward the mansion. To their astonishment, on the site where the mansion should have been, stood a plain house with a simple front porch. McAllister could hardly believe his eyes. The Isle of Hope was in truth one of the most picturesque places in the world, but this house was certainly nothing to boast about. The guide knocked on the door. A servant opened it just a crack.

"When does your master dine?" McAllister inquired.

"Six o'clock."

McAllister asked what was on the menu for that day.

"Pea pie."

"What is pea pie?"

"Cow peas and bacon."

"Then tell your master to kill his fattest turkey, as he will be joined by four hungry friends this afternoon," McAllister commanded.

The servant protested that his master would never permit him to kill such a turkey. McAllister insisted that he and his friends expected a roasted turkey. Just thinking about the dish, McAllister turned to his friends and said, "I have dined on walnut-fed turkey in Florence, Italy, and turkey at Windsor Castle, braised by Her Majesty's chef. None of it compared to a Savannah turkey. You shall see."

Finally McAllister and his party were invited inside, where they could hear Jones ranting and raving about the uninvited guests. When Jones came into the room, he was surprised to see his old acquaintance. "Oh, McAllister, it is you."

The men visited together as the servant prepared the meal. When dinner was announced, the guests were led into the dining room where McAllister expected to view a sideboard heavy with English silver and Waterford crystal. They were seated around a small table and served rice, pea pie, and a roasted turkey. Jones brought forth a bottle of fine old Madeira, which he referred to as "the blood of my ancestors." McAllister's eyes took in every piece of furniture in the room. There was no sideboard at all, and no evidence of any past dinner party having been given in that room. It was clear that while in residence at his magnificent home in Newport, Rhode Island, Mr. Jones of Savannah was simply a boastful planter.

Where "Jingle Bells" Still Lives

During the early 1800s, John Pierpont—orator, poet, author, merchant, lawyer, preacher, and reformer—sent forth into the world his children. There were six, and they possessed not only education and musical talent, but social graces and practical skills. Among them were Juliet; William Alston; John, Jr; and James. As young adults John and James left Boston, where their father—whose literary associates included Whittier, Holmes, Dana, and other figures of the New England renaissance—had established the Pierponts as a sort of dynasty.

It was not surprising that John, Jr., and James ended up in the South, for their father had spent part of his younger life there, and he related stories about that magical place—where people wrote glowing hand-penned notes and made an art of their Low Country society.

John Pierpont graduated from Yale in 1804, one of his classmates having been John C. Calhoun. After assisting for a short time at an academy in Connecticut, John went to Georgetown County, South Carolina, and passed nearly four years as a private tutor in the family of Col. William Alston.

Alston, in deference to his wealth and expertise as a rice planter, was referred to as "King Billy." George Washington had visited him and written in his diary about Colonel Alston's home, Clifton, which was "large, new, and elegantly furnished." It stood, Washington wrote, "on a sandy hill, high for the country" with the Colonel's rice fields below along the "Waggamau" (as Washington spelled the *Waccamaw* River). To Charleston hostesses, Washington had commented that Alston's plantation "looked like fairyland." Servants in the Clifton household wore uniforms of green plush, faced with red and trimmed with silver braid. The Alston carriages bore the family coat of arms.

After his years of tutoring at Clifton, John took the Alston children to Litchfield, Connecticut, where he prepared them for Yale. John's time spent at Clifton was happy, and when his first son was born, he named him William Alston.

John, Jr., followed in his father's footsteps. He attended Harvard Divnity School and was ordained in 1842. Several years later he married Joanna Le Barron Sibley. The young woman died in 1852, having borne no children. It was then that the young man decided to go south. He arrived in Savannah and established himself as a Unitarian minister. His credentials were considered excellent, as his father had forty years earlier been ordained pastor of the Hollis Street Unitarian Church in Boston.

John Pierpont, Jr., needed Savannah as much as Savannah needed him, but he was prone to bouts of homesickness. On May 3, 1852, he wrote

> My dear Father,
>
> How welcome was your letter of 26th ult. as well as the short one I rec'd. . . . Indeed, dear Father, alone as I am in a strange land, a letter from *home* comes as an angel of love to my poor, saddened spirit & I thank you for it. You will not regret the time spent in writing to me if you know what a pleasure it gives me. So, I pray write often.
>
> Well, I am here now fairly located over my new society. 'Tis a strange dream to me, the events of the past month! Away from home & friends—with no dear companion by my side to whom I can confide my sorrows & from whom I can receive consolation—but I must say it, the consciousness that I am not wholly alone, since the *Father* is with me, & I hope & believe also the fine spirit of my wife—still outwardly alone, *wanting*, as I almost hourly do, the sweet communion of some dear friend,—my lot here is as pleasant as I could expect. I have been rec'd with great kindness and cordiality by the Society. So far as I can learn, they hear me gladly. There is not that enthusiasm which New England parishes often manifest towards new ministers, evanescent & unmeaning, vanishing like the morning dew & leaving in the minister's heart nothing

but disappointment & discouragement. But it is, apparently, a healthy cordiality which hopes for its continued existence in the establishment of a perfect confidence between pastor & friend. This I like. . . .

John's letters to his father continued on a regular basis, and he ended them with "love to all" and asked about the welfare of the family. The endings were believed by many who would read the letters in later years to reveal John's despair over the discord between himself and his brother James. James was a musician, and John did not fully approve of his brother's life-style. They became estranged. Although the quarrel between them continued for years, John mentioned James's children in a letter to his father on March 26, 1857. James's wife, Millicent Cowee, had died a few months earlier, leaving three small children.

James continued working as a composer, musician, and music teacher. He wrote songs in the tradition of Stephen Foster, including "Kitty Crow" (a ballad), "I Mourn for My Old Cottage Home," "Ring the Bell Fanny," and "Strike for the South" (a Confederate patriotic song).

A tiny exchange of interest took place while James still lived in Medford, Massachusetts. He called on a friend, Mrs. Otis Waterman, to share with her a tune that had come to mind.

"I have a little song in my head," he told her.

"Please play it for me," she requested.

James sat down at the piano and his fingers flew over the keys.

"That is a merry little jingle," Mrs. Waterman responded with delight.

Soon on his way to Savannah, the young man never gave the "jingle" another thought.

James remarried in 1857, to Eliza Jane Purse. They had five children.

On December 8, 1857, brother John also remarried, to Harriet Louisa Fowler, widow of Dr. George W. Fowler, in Medford, Massachusetts, and carried his new bride back to Georgia. In order to supplement his dwindling income—due to loss of church membership—John joined Charles A. Farley in running a school in Savannah.

On April 8, 1859, John wrote his father with the startling news that he had received a letter from his brother James. He quoted it:

> My dear Brother,
>
> Are you aware that this day is the anniversary of Father's birth? Why should *we*, his children, be estranged? If *Pride* is the barrier, affection leads me to throw it aside, & make the first approach towards a reconciliation. Will you respond?
>
> Truly & affectionately,
> Yr. Brother James.

Thus, brothers John and James Pierpont were reconciled, John stating he believed in the reformation of his brother.

John, soon after, left the school and Unitarian Church in Savannah and moved to Macon, Georgia, where he went into factorial business with his brother-in-law. He continued to be associated with the church, playing the organ for both the Presbyterian and Episcopal congregations.

Elder brother William Alston Pierpont, either despite or because of his father's belief in total abstinence, became an alcoholic. He drifted from town to town and job to job, finally settling in Savannah. William died an alcoholic at the age of fifty. John, Jr., wrote of the death to his father:

> My dear Father,
>
> Yes! Father, poor William has left us, at a time when it seemed as if there was nothing more left for him. Always a generous & kind-hearted man, he has lived & died a poor man—died with no reasonable prospects for the future. I mourn his death for he was a brother whom, notwithstanding the weaknesses incident to & *inherited* in our nature, I loved dearly. That his death was hastened by an intemperate use of spirits & tobacco we cannot but suppose; but I do not believe he died of delirium. . . .

Juliet Pierpont, sister of John and James, married Junius Morgan, son of wealthy businessman Joseph Morgan. They lived in a modest brick cottage on Asylum Street in Hartford, Connecticut. It was in that house on April 17, 1837, that the first of their five children, John Pierpont Morgan, was born. J. P. Morgan became a noted financier.

No one knows the exact date that James Pierpont first heard the familiar notes of the little song he had written so many years earlier in Massachusetts and played for Mrs. Waterman. The "merry little jingle" had miraculously become a popular Christmas tune and been given the name "Jingle Bells." James was not the sort of man who swaggered with an air of braggadocio, but he was always eager to hear the song. A faint tremor of amusement spread on his lips each time he recognized the first notes being played.

James Pierpont died in 1894. He, his wife Eliza, and two of their five children are buried at Laurel Grove Cemetery in Savannah. James Pierpont's grave site is visited by thousands of people each year, in honor of one of the most popular songs ever written: "Jingle Bells."

Walking Egypt

Not so long ago, Wilmington Island, near Savannah, was a remote spot, covered in tropical growth. A place of great natural beauty, it was home to several species of palmetto trees: the dwarf palmetto, the blue palmetto, the saw palmetto, and—most prolific—the cabbage palmetto. The curious bark of this unique tree looks like a rough cover built by carpenters to protect the tree trunk. The bark is, however, formed by nature, and it does indeed protect the trunk, which contains an edible substance. Palmetto cabbage, as the substance is called, is taken from the core of the tree, about a foot below the top. Palmetto cabbage is actually the bud of the tree, white in color, tender, and resembling the ordinary northern cabbage plant. It may be consumed, cooked or uncooked.

During the days following World War II, two young men who had returned from the War were making their way from North Carolina to Florida and found themselves hopelessly lost on Wilmington Island. They survived by eating palmetto cabbage, and to this day they testify that it was delicious. (Of course, they were very hungry.) Wilmington Islanders enjoy it as well. "Palmetto cabbage is good eatin'," said a native. "Jes cut it up and eat it raw. Or you kin cook it up wid fatback." The palmetto tree is used in a variety of other purposes. The fibre endures and is perfect for making rugs, baskets, hats, and other objects.

The people living on Wilmington Island fifty years ago were devoutly religious. They participated in special services in which they "walked Egypt."

One such service was held one night in a small, fairy tale–like praise house on the island. The service began with a prayer. Afterward, a sister stood up, held her hands toward heaven, and prayed, "Oh, Lord, here's givin' You thanks for the blessin' You store on us. We be nuthin' but law-breakers against Your will." Tears rolled down her cheeks as she challenged God to take a sword and cut sin from right to left if He found anything not planted by His own hand "lurkin' round any heart."

After the prayer, a young woman stood to sing. The other worshippers quieted down. This girl was a favorite with them as she was learning to "bring the babies," and she was a take-charge sort of *granny woman*. Her lyrical soprano voice struck a high minor key. Her body began to sway, this way and that. Another woman joined her and, with body swaying, picked up the pitch and sang alto. After that, one and then another among the worshippers stood until all in the small church were joined in the anthem. When the song was concluded, they settled themselves on the crude benches.

Some worshippers were just arriving at the praise house as the song ended. Each new arrival bowed, scraped his or her feet, and shook hands with those already there. Greetings such as "Huddy? [How are you?] How's yer lady?" followed.

The young singer stood again, and without announcement began to sing "Roll, Jordan, Roll," the grandest of all their hymns. Other worshippers joined her, and there was a great rolling sound throughout the small building.

> Oh, roll, Jordan, roll!
> Oh, roll, Jordan, roll!
> My soul arise at heab'n, Lord,
> Fur to hear de Jordan roll!
>
> Little chil'en, learn to fear de Lord,
> And let your days be long,
> Oh, roll, Jordan! Roll, Jordan!
> Roll, Jordan, roll!
>
> Oh, march, angel, march!
> Oh, march, angel, march!
> My soul arise in heab'n, Lord,
> Fur to hear de Jordan roll!

And then the walk to Egypt began.

Worshippers filed up to the pulpit and formed a ring around it. Chanting original prayers and petitions, they pranced around, their bodies jerking and their breath short with emotional frenzy.

Around and around the pulpit they went, their hands on the shoulders of the one in front, their feet beating a monotonous rhythm to the spiritual they were singing. The vibrations from their shouting and dancing shook the fragile building as they clapped, stomped, and shouted.

Oblivious to a weakening floor, the circle went on, unbroken. The movement took its toll on the floor, which was sagging more than ever. Suddenly, it gave way, and all the worshippers crashed through. They didn't seem to notice—and continued to walk Egypt. They went on until they dropped with exhaustion and lay prostrate on the ground.

The Boat Race

Like horse racing, boating afforded the cotton and rice planters ample opportunity for betting. Betting always accompanied the sport and appeared to help promote it. Almost everyone had a wager of some sort at the regattas—"ranging from a cigar, a glass of toddy, a beaver hat, a pair of Durfee's best made boots, or from $100 to $500." Generally in the regular boat club regattas, a purse of considerable size went to the winner, and at several regattas some of the sailing boats were put up as stakes for the wagers.

The first boat clubs formed in the North. As early as 1811 in New York the Knickerbocker Club had come into existence. The Knickerbocker died gradually, but was followed in 1830 by an even more pretentious club.

Among the yachts built in the antebellum South was one launched in 1840 from a Mississippi River plantation thirty-six miles south of New Orleans in the Delta. The yacht's owner, who paid $10,000 for its construction, challenged to a race any boat in New York.

And so it was that sea island cotton planters and rice planters became lovers of water sports and frequently held regattas in Savannah.

Dick Aiken, a rice planter from Darien finally succumbed to the sailing bug and had a yacht built to his specifications. He commissioned for the task master craftsman Charles Floyd. Floyd, who lived on his plantation at nearby St. Marys, Georgia, prided himself on the workmanship of his boats. Although he built for others, he retained a feeling of artistic paternity for those boats he constructed.

When Aiken's yacht was completed, it was the finest on the seas, he believed—a vessel that could outrace any other. One day, while in Savannah, he met Ludlow Cohen, a fertilizer dealer from Charleston, who also owned a crack racing vessel. Both Aiken and

Cohen, open to a challenge, extolled their boats' merits. After further conversation in the presence of others, it was agreed that the men would race their boats on the Vernon River, along the property of John Anderson, at Beaulieu, situated at the mouth of the river in Chatham County.

The day of the race finally arrived, and a large number of spectators congregated around the dock. Aiken and Cohen were excited and more than a little nervous. Aiken's son was in charge of the stake boat, which he immediately took to the strategic point of turn-around, a little over two miles from the starting point. Each man made a last-minute check of the boats, then glanced at the sky. A few cirrus clouds had gathered in the west. They would be running before the wind. The race was considered evenly matched by the crowd gathered at the waterside and all bets had been made by the time the boats set out on the triangular course.

They were off.

Cohen's yacht took the lead from the beginning. By the time he had reached the stake boat, Aiken had fallen behind. Cohen was well on is way back to Beaulieu when the wind suddenly died. Both boats drifted, at the mercy of an occasional breeze. When they finally returned to the landing, a decision had been made by the spectators: another race should be run. Aiken and Cohen walked away from one another, Cohen remarking that he refused to race Aiken again as the fellow was no gentleman.

Aiken did not hear the remark, but Benny Ferrill, a close friend of Aiken, did. Ferrill asked Cohen what he meant by such a disparaging statement.

"His son moved the stake boat to Aiken's advantage," Cohen accused.

Ferrill suggested a second race and told Cohen that, if he didn't take back what he had said, Aiken would be told of the remark.

Cohen was furious. He balled up a fist and hit his other palm with it. "Then tell him!"

Ferrill flew into the Anderson house, located Aiken, and repeated to him Cohen's accusation. Ferrill and Aiken discussed a challenge, and when they decided to proceed with it, Aiken dictated the dare to Ferrill, who wrote it in a great hurry.

Aiken took the paper from Ferrill, approached Cohen, and read aloud the challenge that demanded a full retraction and apology in lieu of a meeting with Cohen's choice of weapons.

Cohen's friends attempted to talk him out of pursuing the challenge, trying to convince him that although he might be the better yachtsman, Aiken was more skilled in the use of firearms. Their words fell on deaf ears. Cohen felt backed into a corner and decided he must prove himself.

Pistols made in London were selected as weapons.

Friends continued to try to calm Aiken and Cohen, but to no avail. When the two men attempted to select "seconds," many of their friends refused. Finally, the seconds were chosen: Ferrill would act for Aiken and Capt. David Waldhauer, a member of the Georgia Hussars who had lost an arm at Gettysburg during the Civil War, agreed to act for Cohen. Dr. William Duncan and Dr. Thomas J. Charlton, surgeons, consented to be at the scene in case they were needed.

The duel was deemed important enough to be fought on ground of honor, and because of this the discussion regarding the site was a lengthy one. Brampton Plantation was decided upon, as Cohen and his friends were acquainted with the owner, Dr. James Bond Read.

Throughout the colonial era Brampton Plantation was known commonly as "Jonathan Bryan's Plantation." In 1765 the plantation had its beginning when Bryan purchased from Thomas Vincent, for his wife Mary and their daughter Ann, the lower 250 acres of Vincent's estate. The plantation was named Brampton for the ancestral home of the Bryans in England. The proximity of the tract to Savannah and its beautiful small bluff made it an ideal site for a home. Jonathan Bryan was a man of enormous physique, described as a "tall and large man of wonderful strength and hardihood, and of imposing appearance." His wedding vest, of heavy white taffeta, elegantly embroidered with tiny rosebuds and green vines, was displayed many years later in a Savannah museum. It dwarfed other garments exhibited beside it.

The Williamson family later owned Brampton, but destruction wrought by Sherman's soldiers and southern sympathizers during the Civil War left the owner financially ruined. A torch was put to the residence, but the owner managed to salvage two fine mantels from the drawing room. The plantation was sold in 1867 to Dr. James Bond Read of Savannah, who owned it at the time of the duel between Ludlow Cohen and Dick Aiken. The beautiful small bluff, which had originally attracted Jonathan Bryan to the place, was to be the setting for the confrontation. Brampton was uninhabited at the time.

As the party assembled on the bluff at the appointed hour, Aiken and Cohen showed signs of having spent a restless night. They nodded cold salutations to each other. When the choice of positions fell to Cohen, he selected the east. No attempts at reconciliation were made.

The usual procedure in such a duel followed that after each exchange of shots the "seconds" would try to work out an accord by which the men could be reconciled. This was not done, however, and a volley of shots rang out. Neither man was hit. Pistols were reloaded, and the determined men again squeezed the triggers. On the fifth exchange of shots, Cohen's right arm went limp. The surgeons ran to examine him and proclaimed that the wound would very likely be fatal. Cohen died at 3:00 PM that day. His remains were returned to Charleston for burial.

Although the event was Savannah's last fatal duel, the episode was one of flammable stuff. Some said that after an exchange of shots when neither party was hit, it was the duty of the "second" of the challengee to face the other "second" and ask if that side was satisfied. Others believed that one and certainly two shots should satisfy any man's honor.

The Charleston *Courier* reported "The deceased was well known here as a young gentleman of high tone and character."

The question of which man had the fastest sailboat was never settled.

BREADS

Charleston Banana Boat Bread

1 cup shortening
2 cups sugar
4 eggs
6 ripe bananas
2-1/2 cups cake flour
1 teaspoon salt
2 teaspoons baking soda

Cream shortening and sugar. Beat eggs and add to creamed mixture. Mash bananas and add. Sift flour, salt, and soda together three times and blend into mixture. Do not overmix. Bake at 350 degrees 50 minutes. Makes 2 loaves.

Cranberry Lemon Nut Bread

1/4 cup shortening
3/4 cup sugar
1 egg
1-1/3 cups milk
3 cups all-purpose flour
3-1/2 teaspoons baking powder
1 teaspoon salt
1 cup chopped nuts
1 cup cranberries, rinsed, drained, and cut in half
grated rind of 1 lemon
1 teaspoon ground mace

Cream shortening and sugar. Beat in egg. Stir in milk. Add flour, baking powder, and salt; beat until smooth and thick. Fold in nuts, cranberries, lemon rind, and mace. Bake in 3 small tins at 350 degrees for 55 minutes.

Zucchini Bread

3 eggs
1 cup vegetable oil
2 cups sugar
2 teaspoons vanilla extract
2 cups shredded, unpeeled zucchini
1 8-1/2-ounce can crushed pineapple, drained
3 cups all-purpose flour
2 teaspoons baking soda
1-1/2 teaspoon ground cinnamon
1 teaspoon salt
3/4 teaspoon ground nutmeg
1/4 teaspoon baking powder
1 cup chopped dates
1 cup chopped pecans

Beat together eggs, oil, sugar, and vanilla. Stir in remaining ingredients; mix well. Turn into two greased 9-by-5-inch loaf pans. Bake at 350 degrees about 1 hour.

Cranberry Muffins

1 cup all-purpose flour, sifted
1/2 cup sugar
3/4 teaspoon baking powder
1/4 teaspoon baking soda
1/2 teaspoon salt
2 tablespoons butter
1/2 cup orange juice
1/2 teaspoon grated orange peel
1 egg, beaten
1/2 cup coarsely chopped fresh cranberries
1/4 cup chopped nuts

Sift dry ingredients together in bowl. Cut in butter. In a separate bowl, combine juice, orange peel, and egg. Add juice mixture to dry ingredients, blending only enough to moisten. Fold in cranberries and nuts. Fill greased muffin tins about two-thirds full. Bake at 350 for 15 minutes. Yields 12.

Sweet Potato Muffins

3 cups cooked sweet potatoes
4 tablespoons butter
1/2 cup sugar
1 egg
1/4 cup all-purpose flour
2 teaspoons baking powder
1/2 teaspoon salt
1/2 teaspoon cinnamon
1/4 teaspoon nutmeg
1/2 cup milk
4 tablespoons chopped walnuts
4 tablespoons raisins

Puree sweet potatoes in a food processor or blender. Cream butter and sugar. Beat in the egg and potatoes. Sift flour with baking powder, salt, cinnamon, and nutmeg; add alternately by hand with milk, nuts, and raisins. Mix until blended. Do not overmix. Spoon into greased muffin tins, filling each completely full. A little sugar and cinnamon may be sprinkled on top of each muffin. Bake at 400 degrees for 25 minutes. [Yummy served with hot apple juice.] Yields 30 muffins.

Orange Blossom Muffins

1 egg, slightly beaten
1/2 cup sugar
1-1/2 cup orange juice
1 tablespoon vegetable oil
2 cups all-purpose flour
1 teaspoon salt
3 teaspoons baking powder
1/2 cup orange marmalade
1/2 cup chopped pecans

Combine egg, sugar, juice, and oil. Add dry ingredients; beat together well. Stir in marmalade and pecans. Grease muffin pans. Bake at 400 degrees for 25 minutes. Yields 16 muffins.

Morning Glory Muffins

1 cup Fiber One cereal, crushed in blender
1/3 cup milk
1-3/4 cups all-purpose flour
3/4 cup chopped apple
1/2 cup brown sugar, packed
1/2 cup finely shredded carrots
1/4 cup granulated sugar
1/4 cup flaked coconut
1/4 cup vegetable oil
2 eggs
3 tablespoons baking powder
2 teaspoons ground cinnamon
1 teaspoon vanilla extract
1/2 teaspoon salt

Grease bottoms only of 12 medium muffin cups, 2-1/2-by-1-1/4 inches, or line muffin pan with baking cups. Mix cereal and milk in large bowl; let stand about 5 minutes—until cereal is softened. Sift baking powder, flour, and salt together three times. [This step is very important.] Add remaining ingredients to cereal and milk and stir until blended. Fill muffin cups almost full. Bake at 400 degrees 22 to 25 minutes or until golden brown. Remove immediately from pan.

• *Morning Glory Muffins with Smucker's Black Raspberry Jam and coffee is a wonderful start of my day. NR*

Bran Refrigerator Muffins

great for breakfast

**2 cups boiling water
4 cups Kellogg's All Bran
2 cups Nabisco 100% Bran
1 quart buttermilk
1 cup shortening
3 cups sugar
4 eggs
5 cups all-purpose flour
5 teaspoons baking soda
1 teaspoon salt**

Pour water over bran. Stir in buttermilk. Let mixture stand while creaming together shortening and sugar. Beat eggs into creamed mixture one at a time. Add creamed mixture to bran. Sift flour, measure, sift again with soda and salt. Add flour to batter, stirring just enough to dampen dry ingredients. Do not overstir. Fill muffin tins two-thirds full. Bake at 375 degrees for 15 to 25 minutes, until slightly brown on top. Yields 2-1/2 dozen muffins. [Muffins freeze well.]

Cornbread

1 cup yellow plain cornmeal
1 cup all-purpose flour
3 teaspoons sugar
1 teaspoon baking powder
1/4 teaspoon salt
1/4 cup oil
1 cup skim milk
2 eggs, beaten

Combine dry ingredients in a bowl. Add oil, milk, and eggs, stirring only until flour is moistened. Do not overmix. Pour into a greased 8-by-8-inch pan. Bake at 400 degrees for 25 minutes. Serves 6.

Cornbread #2

3-1/4 cups all-purpose flour
2 cups white plain cornmeal
1-1/4 cups powdered milk
3 tablespoons baking powder
1/4 cup sugar
1-1/2 teaspoons salt
2/3 cup shortening
3 large eggs
3-2/3 cups water
1/8 teaspoon yellow food coloring (optional)

In a large bowl, combine flour, cornmeal, powdered milk, baking powder, sugar, and salt. Melt shortening. Beat eggs and water together; add melted shortening and food coloring. Add egg mixture to dry ingredients and stir until all ingredients are combined. Pour into two 9-inch greased pans and bake at 400 degrees for 30 minutes.

Mexican Cornbread

1/2 pound sausage
3 teaspoons baking powder
2 teaspoons sugar
1 teaspoon salt
1-1/2 cups plain cornmeal
1/2 11-ounce can Mexican style corn, drained
1/2 cup all-purpose flour, sifted
1 egg
3 tablespoons melted butter
3/4 cup buttermilk
1/4 cup canned green chili peppers, drained and diced

Fry sausage; save drippings. Sift together flour, baking powder, sugar, and salt; combine with cornmeal. Mix together egg, butter, and buttermilk; blend in dry ingredients. Stir in corn chilis and sausage. Bake in 9-1/2-inch round cake pan at 400 degrees for 25 minutes. Serves 6.

Southern Spoon Bread

Every Southern cook serves spoon bread.
It is especially good when served with a fruit salad.

3 cups milk
1 cup cornmeal
1 teaspoon salt
4 eggs, separated
2-1/2 teaspoons baking powder

Heat milk in double boiler. Add salt. Gradually stir in cornmeal and cook until smooth. Remove from heat and cool completely. Beat in baking powder and egg yolks. Fold in beaten egg whites. Turn into greased 12-by-8-by-2-inch casserole and place in pan of water in oven. [Some cooks bake in greased custard cups.] Bake at 375 degrees about 35 minutes. Serves 8.

Popovers

1 cup all-purpose flour, sifted
1/4 teaspoon salt
2 eggs, beaten
1 cup milk
2 tablespoons shortening, melted

Sift flour and salt together. Combine eggs, milk, and shortening; gradually add to flour mixture, beating about 1 minute. Fill greased, heated muffin tins three-quarters full and bake in very hot oven (450 degrees) about 20 minutes. Reduce heat to 350 degrees and continue baking 20 minutes. Yields 8.

Angel Biscuits

1 package dry yeast
2 tablespoons lukewarm water
5 cups all-purpose flour
1 teaspoon salt
3 tablespoons baking powder
5 tablespoons sugar
1 cup shortening
2 cups buttermilk with 1 teaspoon baking soda added

Dissolve yeast in water. Mix 4 cups flour and remaining dry ingredients; cut in shortening. Add yeast and buttermilk to flour and mix well. Mixture will be moist. Slowly add last cup of flour. Turn out onto lightly floured surface and knead—pressing, folding, and stretching—for 2 minutes. Roll to desired thickness and cut with floured biscuit cutter. Bake in greased biscuit pan at 400 degrees until golden brown, 12 to 15 minutes. Yields 2 pans of biscuits. [Dough stores well in refrigerator for several days. If you don't wish to make the whole recipe at once, pinch off what you need.]

Beaufort Buttermilk Light Rolls

2 tablespoons sugar
4 tablespoons shortening
1 package dry yeast
1/2 cup warm water
2 cups buttermilk
5 cups all-purpose flour
1 teaspoon baking soda
1 teaspoon baking powder
1 teaspoon salt

Cream sugar and shortening. Dissolve yeast in water in a 1-cup measuring cup; add enough buttermilk to fill the cup. Set aside. Sift 2 cups flour with the other dry ingredients; stir in yeast mixture, adding alternately with remaining buttermilk. Work in the additional 3 cups of flour to make a soft dough. Put dough in bowl and place in refrigerator. It will rise quickly once it has been thoroughly chilled (approximately 3 hours). The longer it stays in refrigerator, the better the rolls. [But don't let it stay in long enough to begin drying out.] Form cold dough into balls and place on baking sheet. Allow rolls to rise 1 hour before baking. Bake at 400 degrees for 20 minutes. Yields about 8 dozen.

BEVERAGES

During the Colonial era, when the genteel tee-totaling woman desired a fizz in her beverage and she felt daring enough, she added ginger ale.

Banana Punch

6 cups water
3 cups sugar
3 cups crushed pineapple
2 cups orange juice
3 large bananas, mashed
2 2-liter bottles lemon lime soda, Sprite, or ginger ale

Mix together all ingredients except soda. Put in freezer for 20 hours. Add soda just before serving. Great! Serves 15.

Wassail

1 64-ounce bottle apple juice
1/2 cup liquid cinnamon

Heat; keep hot in crock. Serve with a dollop of Cool Whip or a slice of orange on top. Serves 15.

Strawberry Punch

1 cup frozen strawberries, thawed
1 20-ounce can crushed pineapple
1 cup sugar
juice of 2 lemons
1 2-liter ginger ale
ice cubes

Stir all together. Serve cold. Serves 15.

Russian Tea

juice of 2 lemons, reserving rinds
juice of 3 oranges, reservings rinds
12 whole cloves
1 quart water
2 cups sugar
2 quarts strong tea

Boil water, cloves, and rinds for 5 minutes. Drain and add sugar, juices, and tea. Serve piping hot. Yields 2-1/2 quarts.
• *This is the tea served to President and Mrs. Nixon many years ago when they visited the mother of Billy Graham in Charlotte.* NR

Christmas/Valentine Punch

4 64-ounce bottles Whitehouse apple juice
2 16-ounce cans pineapple juice
1 can frozen orange juice
3 bottles cinnamon candy (the little red candy in spice section)

Dilute orange juice as directed on can. Mix with other ingredients, heat, and serve. [If served cold, let stand a few hours until candy melts.] Serves 40 to 50.

Lemon Delight

2-1/2 cups sugar
2/3 cup water
grated rind and juice of 6 lemons
1 quart water
1 2-liter bottle ginger ale

Put sugar in 2/3 cup water to dissolve. Let stand 30 minutes. Add 1 quart water and lemon. Stir in ginger ale just before serving. Yields about 1 gallon.

Coffee Punch

1 quart heavy cream, chilled
5 tablespoons confectioners sugar
5 teaspoons vanilla extract
2 quarts vanilla ice cream
1 gallon black coffee, chilled

Whip cream until almost stiff. Add sugar and vanilla and whip until it holds shape. Place whipped cream and scoops of ice cream in punch bowl. Pour coffee over and mix well. Serves 50 to 60.

Coffee Punch #2

1 quart strong coffee
1/2 pint cream
1 pint vanilla ice cream
5 teaspoons vanilla extract
5 tablespoons sugar

Chill coffee. Whip cream and add sugar and vanilla. Place ice cream and whipped cream in punch bowl and pour coffee over it. Mix well before serving. Serves 25.

Festival Punch

3 quarts apple juice
1 quart low-calorie cranberry juice cocktail
1 2-liter bottle sugar-free ginger ale

Combine juices and refrigerate at least 5 hours. Chill ginger ale. When ready to serve, place an ice ring or crushed ice in punch bowl and add juice. Pour in ginger ale and stir. Serves about 35.

"CANNED" GOODS

Sid's Chow Chow

24 peppers, red and green
12 onions
boiling water
5 cups vinegar
5 cups sugar
1-1/2 tablespoons salt
2 tablespoons mustard seed

Grind peppers and onions and cover with boiling water. Let stand 5 minutes. Drain well. Combine remaining ingredients and bring to boil over medium heat. Add peppers and onions; allow to boil 10 minutes. Seal in sterilized jars while mixture is hot.

Sid's Tomato Catsup

1/2 bushel tomatoes, unpeeled
boiling water
2 tablespoons salt (more or less, as desired)
2 tablespoons black pepper
1/2 teaspoon cayenne pepper
2 tablespoons pickling spices
3 pints apple cider vinegar
2 pounds brown sugar

Pour boiling water over tomatoes. Quarter tomatoes and boil 20 minutes or until they can be run through a sieve. Combine tomatoes with remaining ingredients and boil until thick. Seal in sterilized jars while mixture is hot.

Zucchini Pickles

2 pounds (approximately 6) small zucchini squash, unpeeled
4 small white onions
1-1/2 tablespoons slacked lime
6-1/2 cups cold water
2-1/2 cups apple cider vinegar
1 to 1-1/2 cups sugar
2 teaspoons salt
1/2 teaspoon ground ginger
1 clove garlic
1 stick cinnamon
1 teaspoon whole allspice
hot red peppers (1 for each jar)
1/2 teaspoon celery seed
1/2 teaspoon mustard seed

Wash, rinse, drain, and cut zucchini into 1/8 to 1/4-inch slices. Skin, wash, and slice onions. Put vegetables together in large bowl. Thoroughly mix lime with water and pour over zucchini and onions. Add more water if needed to cover. Put a plate inside bowl to insure vegetables are immersed. Refrigerate 5 to 6 hours. Remove vegetables from bowl, rinse in cold water, and drain.

Put vinegar, sugar, salt, and ginger in pot. Tie garlic, cinnamon, and allspice in a piece of cheesecloth and add to vinegar mixture. Boil until sugar dissolves. Reduce heat and simmer 10 to 15 minutes. Remove and discard spices. Taste; add more salt if desired.

Put onion and zucchini in pot and boil 3 to 4 minutes. Vegetables must be hot through but not cooked. While hot, pack slices in pint fruit jars. Add tiny hot pepper to each jar when about half filled with vegetables. When jars filled to one-half inch from top, add celery seed and mustard seed. Bring vinegar mixture to hard boil and pour over vegetables. Seal jars while hot.

24-Hour Pickles

7 pounds cucumbers (about a dishpan full)
1 small Lilly lime (from drug or grocery store)
2 ounces powdered alum
3 pounds coarse salt (about 2-1/2 cups)
1 1-1/2-ounce box mixed pickling spices
2 quarts sugar
2 quarts apple cider vinegar

Slice cucumbers thin. Dissolve lime in water and soak cucumbers 12 hours. Drain and rinse in 3 changes of cold water. Soak in salted water 4 hours. Drain and rinse in 3 changes of cold water. Cover with cold water and alum; simmer for about 5 minutes—NOT MORE THAN 5 MINUTES. Drain and rinse in hot water. Pour in pot with vinegar, sugar, and spices; simmer 30 minutes. Remove from heat and let stand to room temperature. Pack by hand and seal.
[NOTE: Do not use aluminum in preparing this recipe.]

Watermelon Rind Pickles

Use 10 pounds of watermelon rind with all green and red removed. Cut in strips measuring about 3/4 inch wide by 2 inches long. Soak strips in water into which 2 cups of slacked lime has been dissolved, using a glass or plastic container (not aluminum or other metal) overnight. The following day, remove strips, wash, and rinse 2 times in cold water. Put pickles in a large pot, cover with water, and salt to taste. Boil 20 minutes. Remove strips, wash, and rinse in cold water. Put strips in clear water and boil 20 minutes. Remove from pot, wash, and rinse in cold water.

SYRUP

8 pounds sugar
3 pints white vinegar
1 1-1/4-ounce box whole cloves
1 1-1/4-ounce box whole allspice
several drops red or green food coloring

Dissolve sugar in vinegar in large pot. Tie spices in clean white cheesecloth and drop into vinegar. Add food coloring. Boil pickles in vinegar mixture about 1-1/2 hours—until a toothpick is easily inserted. DO NOT OVERCOOK. Some rinds will be thicker than others. Cook until the thick ones are ready. Put in sterilized jars and seal. Before using, put a jar in refrigerator for about 2 days and chill.

Sid's 13-Days-But-Worth-It Pickles

• FIRST DAY
Wash and pack **whole, small cucumbers** in glass gallon jars. Add 1 cup **salt** to each gallon. Cover cucumbers with **boiling water**.

• SECOND DAY
Drain and rinse cucumbers with hot water. Cover with boiling water to which 3 ounces of **alum** have been added.

• THIRD DAY
Drain, rinse, and cover cucumbers with boiling water.

• FOURTH DAY
Drain and cover cucumbers with 2 quarts (or whatever is needed to cover) **boiling vinegar**. Add 1/2 **1-1/2-ounce box pickling spices** to jar. Be sure cucumbers are covered. Let stand until 13th day.

• THIRTEENTH DAY
Drain cucumbers. Discard liquid. Cut cucumbers in pieces, as desired. Layer cucumbers, sugar, cucumbers, sugar, until you have used 5 pounds of **sugar** per gallon jar or all cucumber pieces are fully covered in sugar. Let stand in jar and use as needed. The jars do not have to be sealed.

• *These pickles are better if they have been refrigerated. We remove about a quart or two of pickles at a time and keep in the refrigerator in smaller jars. NR*

A

Angel Biscuits, 249
APPETIZERS
 Broiled Grapefruit, 6
 Cheese Ball, 5
 Gazpacho, 6
 Grape Jelly Meat Balls #2, 2
 Ham Rolls, 4
 Health Cocktail, 5
 Party Mix, 4
 Provincial Meat Balls in Grape
  Jelly, 2
 Veggie Pizza, 3
Apple Nut Cake, 174
Apricot Nectar Cake, 177
Aunt Lill's Apricot Acapulco,
 145
Aunt Lill's Mt. Fuji Japanese
 Fruit Cake, 176
Aunt Lill's Salmon
 Saskatchewan, 27
Aunt Lill's Spam Spokane, 66
Aunt Lill's Tomatoes Tivoli, 46

B

Baked Apples, 51
Baked Apples #2, 51
Baked Beans, 56
Baked Beans and Pineapple, 57
Baked Beans Wadmalaw, 57
Baked Chicken, 11
Baked Fruit, 52
Baked Stuffed Potatoes, 47
Banana Cake, 178
Banana Punch, 252
barbecue, 12, 15, 21, 63
Barbecue Sauce, 63
Barbecued Chicken, 12
Barbecued Chicken #2, 12
Barbecued Corned Beef, 15
Beaufort Buttermilk Light Rolls,
 250
BEAUFORT LEGENDS, 28–40
beef, 2, 13–18, 58
BEEF

Barbecued Corned, 15
Beef Noodle Stroganoff, 17
Hotsy-Totsy Beef Stew, 16
London Broil, 18
Planter's Meat Loaf, 15
Spaghetti, 18
Stuffed Green Peppers, 16
Beef Noodle Stroganoff, 17
Benne Cookies, 181
BEVERAGES
 Banana Punch, 252
 Christmas/Valentine Punch,
  253
 Coffee Punch, 254
 Coffee Punch #2, 254
 Festival Punch, 254
 Lemon Delight, 253
 Russian Tea, 253
 Strawberry Punch, 252
 Wassail, 252
"Black Ankle," 206–215
Black Bean Chili, 72
"Blackbeard's Ultimatum," 81–
 85
Blender Bèarnaise Sauce, 64
Blender Hollandaise, 64
"Boat Race, The," 237–240
"Boastful Planter, The," 224–228
Bonnie Doone Plantation
 Thanksgiving Cookies, 181
Bran Refrigerator Muffins, 246
BREADS
 Angel Biscuits, 249
 Beaufort Buttermilk Light
  Rolls, 250
 Bran Refrigerator Muffins, 246
 Charleston Banana Boat, 242
 Cornbread, 247
 Cornbread #2, 247
 Cranberry Lemon Nut, 242
 Cranberry Muffins, 243
 Mexican Cornbread, 248
 Morning Glory Muffins, 245
 Orange Blossom Muffins, 244
 Popovers, 249

Southern Spoon, 248
Sweet Potato Muffins, 244
Zucchini, 243
Broiled Grapefruit, 6
Brown Rice and Oysters, 24

C

CAKES
Apple Nut, 174
Apricot Nectar, 177
Aunt Lill's Mt. Fuji Japanese
Fruit, 176
Banana, 178
Charleston's Lady Baltimore,
167
Chocolate Chip, 169
Chocolate Chips Pound, 169
Glazed French Applesauce,
175
Ice Cream, 172
Indulgent Red Velvet, 168
Lady Baltimore Frosting, 178
Lemon, 179
Marble Top, 170
Poppy Seed, 174
Poppy Seed #2, 175
Seven-Minute White Icing, 178
Sideboard Buttermilk Pound,
172
Sour Cream Pound, 172
Spicy Raisin Coffee, 171
Threefold Chocolate, 170
Candied Yums, 48
CANDIES
Sour Cream Fudge, 154
Strawberries, 154
Uncooked Fudge, 155
"CANNED" GOODS
Sid's Chow Chow, 256
Sid's 13-Days-But-Worth-It
Pickles, 259
Sid's Tomato Catsup, 256
24-Hour Pickles, 258
Watermelon Rind Pickles, 258
Zucchini Pickles, 257

CASSEROLES
Baked Beans, 56
Baked Beans and Pineapple,
57
Baked Beans Wadmalaw, 57
Chicken, 59
Chicken Spaghetti, 59
Chicken Tetrazzini, 60
Coastal Crab, 61
Crabmeat, 61
Eggplant, 55
Glorified English Peas, 54
Ground Beef, 58
Hoppin' John, 54
Macaroni, 58
Rice Consommé, 56
Shrimp Crab, 60
String Bean, 54
Tastee Tomato, 56
Zucchini, 55
Charleston Banana Boat Bread,
242
Charleston's Lady Baltimore
Cake, 167
CHARLESTON LEGENDS, 75–
135
"Charleston's Secret Millionaires
Club," 120–125
Cheese Ball, 5
chicken, 8–13, 59–60, 69
CHICKEN
Baked, 11
Barbecued, 12
Barbecued #2, 12
Chicken and Beef, 13
Chicken and Dumplings, 13
Fried, 9
Fried, and Gravy, 9
Honey-Glazed Fried, 8
Plantation Fried, 10
Simply Baked, 11
Chicken and Beef, 13
Chicken Casserole, 59
Chicken and Dumplings, 13
Chicken Soup, 69

Chicken Spaghetti, 59
Chicken Tetrazzini, 60
Chilled Cucumber Soup, 74
chocolate, 154–155, 162, 169–
  170, 182
Chocolate Chip Cake, 169
Chocolate Chips Pound Cake,
  169
Christmas/Valentine Punch, 253
Coastal Crab Casserole, 61
Coastal Orange Carrot Ring, 44
Coconut Pie Shell, 159
Coffee Punch, 254
Coffee Punch #2, 254
Congealed Fruit Salad, 144
Connoisseur Congealed Salad,
  142
COOKIES
  Benne, 181
  Bonnie Doone Plantation
    Thanksgiving, 181
  Peanut Butter, 182
  Persimmon, 183
  Party Chocolate, 182
Cornbread, 247
Cornbread #2, 247
Crabmeat Casserole, 61
Cranberry Lemon Nut Bread,
  242
Cranberry Muffins, 243
Cranberry Salad, 143
Cucumber Salad, 137

D
"Daughters Were in the Attic,
  The," 113–115
"Day the Press Snitched on
  Charleston's Most Sacred
  Social Organization, The,"
  129–135
DESSERTS
  Aunt Lill's Lemon Lucerne,
    150
  Aunt Lill's Lemon Tea Cakes,
    149

Island Ice Cream Odyssey, 152
Orange Coconut Balls, 151
Raspberry Ice Cream, 151
"Raving Good" Presbyterian
  Gingerbread, 148
Sid's Blueberry Cobbler, 150
"Double Bad Luck Day," 202–
  205
Double Squash Crunch, 42

E
Eggplant Casserole, 55

F
Festival Punch, 254
Fried Chicken, 9
Fried Green Tomatoes, 45
Fried Sweet Potatoes, 49
"Frogmore," 39–40
Frogmore Stew, 26
FRUITS
  Baked Apples, 51
  Baked Apples #2, 51
  Baked Fruit, 52
  Pears in Burgundy Sauce, 52

G
Gazpacho, 6
Georgia Peach Salad, 144
"Ghost of Bonaventure, The,"
  186–192
Ginger Ale Salad, 143
Glazed French Applesauce Cake,
  175
Glazed Pork Roast, 22
Glorified English Peas, 54
Grape Jelly Meat Balls #2, 2
Ground Beef Casserole, 58

H
Ham Rolls, 4
"Haunted House at 76 Meeting
  Street," 126–128
Health Cocktail, 5
Heavenly Orange Fluff, 141

Hell Hole Swamp Mud Pie, 162
Honey-Glazed Fried Chicken, 8
Hoppin' John, 54
Hotsy-Totsy Beef Stew, 16
Hotsy-Totsy Fried Green Tomatoes, 45
"House Built for Love, The," 118–119

I
ice cream, 151–152, 172
Ice Cream Cake, 172
"Indian Hill on St. Helena Island, The," 33–34
Indulgent Red Velvet Cake, 168
"Island that Disappeared, The," 37–38
Island Ice Cream Odyssey, 152
Island Pie, 161
It's-A-Sin Strawberry Pudding, 163

J
Jack-O'-Lantern Soup, 71

K
Key Lime Pie, 161

L
Lady Baltimore Frosting, 178
Lemon Cake, 179
Lemon Delight, 253
London Broil, 18
"Lost at Sea," 109–112

M
"Madam Truth," 216–218
"Man Who Bought Himself Three Times, The," 193–197
Maraschino Soufflé Pie, 159
Marble Top Cake, 170
Marinated Asparagus, 137
Marinated Tomatoes, 139
Mexican Cornbread, 248
Morning Glory Muffins, 245

"Mrs. Habersham's Terrapin Stew," 219–223
"Murder on Meeting Street," 96–103
"Murder Trial of Stephen Denaro, The," 116–117

N
"Narrative of Sam Polite, Slave on St. Helena Island," 35–36

O
Old South Red Rice, 46
Orange Blossom Muffins, 244
Orange Coconut Balls, 151
Orange Jell-O, 141
Oyster Pie, 25
Oyster Stew, 69

P
Party Chocolate Cookies, 182
Party Mix, 4
Peanut Butter Cookies, 182
Peanut Soup, 71
Pears in Burgundy Sauce, 52
Pecan Chiffon Pie, 157
Pecan Pie, 158
Perfect Mashed Potatoes, 47
Persimmon Cookies, 183
Persimmon Pudding, 163
Pickled Beets, 44
pickles, 44, 256–259
PIES & PUDDINGS
    Coconut Pie Shell, 159
    Hell Hole Swamp Mud Pie, 162
    Island Pie, 161
    It's-A-Sin Strawberry Pudding, 163
    Key Lime Pie, 161
    Maraschino Soufflé Pie, 159
    Pecan Chiffon Pie, 157
    Pecan Pie, 158
    Persimmon Pudding, 163
    Two-Crust Cherry Pie, 160

"Pirates Who Slipped and Fell, The," 94–95
Plantation Fried Chicken, 10
Planter's Meat Loaf, 15
Popovers, 249
Poppy Seed Cake, 174
Poppy Seed Cake #2, 175
PORK
  Glazed Pork Roast, 22
  Saucy Pineapple Pork Chops, 20
  Spare the Ribs Barbecue, 21
  Sweet-Sour Spareribs, 21
Potato Soup, 73
Provincial Meat Balls in Grape Jelly, 2

Q

R
"Rebellion," 104–108
Red Cabbage Slaw, 42
rice, 46, 56
Rice Consommé, 56
"Riddle of the Broad River Sphinx, The," 31–32
Russian Tea, 253

S
SALADS
  Aunt Lill's Apricot Acapulco, 145
  Congealed Fruit, 144
  Connoisseur Congealed, 142
  Cranberry, 143
  Cucumber, 137
  Georgia Peach, 144
  Ginger Ale, 143
  Heavenly Orange Fluff, 141
  Marinated Asparagus, 137
  Marinated Tomatoes, 139
  Orange Jell-O, 141
  Spaghetti, 139
  Spinach, 138
  Strawberry, 140
  Sweet Dressing for Fruit, 146
  Tomato Aspic, 138
  Vinegar, 140
  Watermelon Fruit, 146
Salmon Patties, 27
SANDWICHES
  Aunt Lill's Spam Spokane, 66
  Vegetable, 66
SAUCES
  Barbecue, 63
  Blender Bèarnaise, 64
  Blender Hollandaise, 64
  Simple Barbecue, 63
Saucy Pineapple Pork Chops, 20
SAVANNAH LEGENDS, 184–240
seafood, 24–27, 60–61, 69–70
SEAFOOD
  Aunt Lill's Salmon Saskatchewan, 27
  Brown Rice and Oysters, 24
  Frogmore Stew, 26
  Oyster Pie, 25
  Salmon Patties, 27
  Shrimp Creole, 25
Seven-Minute White Icing, 178
She Crab Soup, 70
Sherried Acorn Squash, 42
Shrimp Crab Casserole, 60
Shrimp Creole, 25
Sid's Chow Chow, 256
Sid's 13-Days-But-Worth-It Pickles, 259
Sid's Tomato Catsup, 256
Sideboard Buttermilk Pound Cake, 172
Simple Barbecue Sauce, 63
Simply Baked Chicken, 11
SOUPS
  Black Bean Chili, 72
  Chicken, 69
  Chilled Cucumber, 74
  Jack-O'-Lantern, 71
  Oyster Stew, 69
  Peanut, 71

Potato, 73
She Crab, 70
Tideline Oyster Stew, 70
Tomato, 72
Tomato #2, 73
Turkey Vegetable, 68
Sour Cream Fudge, 154
Sour Cream Pound Cake, 172
Southern Spoon Bread, 248
Spaghetti Salad, 139
Spare the Ribs Barbecue, 21
"Speculation on Margaret
    Mitchell," 86–93
Spicy Raisin Coffee Cake, 171
Spinach Salad, 138
Strawberries, 154
Strawberry Punch, 252
Strawberry Salad, 140
String Bean Casserole, 54
Stuffed Green Peppers, 16
Stuffed Squash, 42
Sweet Dressing for Fruit Salad,
    146
Sweet Potato Muffins, 244
Sweet Potatoes in Orange Cups,
    48
Sweet-Sour Spareribs, 21

T
Tastee Tomato, 56
Threefold Chocolate Cake, 170
Tideline Oyster Stew, 70
Tomato Aspic, 138
Tomato Soup, 72
Tomato Soup #2, 73
tomatoes, 6, 45–46, 56, 72–73,
    138–139
Turkey Vegetable Soup, 68
24-Hour Pickles, 258
"Twilight Club, The," 29–30
Two-Crust Cherry Pie, 160

U
Uncooked Fudge, 155

V
Vegetable Sandwiches, 66
VEGETABLES
    Aunt Lill's Tomatoes Tivoli,
        46
    Baked Stuffed Potatoes, 47
    Candied Yums, 48
    Coastal Orange Carrot Ring,
        44
    Double Squash Crunch, 42
    Fried Green Tomatoes, 45
    Fried Sweet Potatoes, 48
    Hotsy-Totsy Fried Green
        Tomatoes, 45
    Old South Red Rice, 46
    Perfect Mashed Potatoes, 47
    Pickled Beets, 44
    Red Cabbage Slaw, 42
    Sherried Acorn Squash, 42
    Stuffed Squash, 42
    Sweet Potatoes in Orange
        Cups, 49
Veggie Pizza, 3
Vinegar Salad, 140

W
"Walking Egypt," 234–236
Wassail, 252
Watermelon Fruit Salad, 146
Watermelon Rind Pickles, 258
"Where 'Jingle Bells' Still
    Lives," 229–233
"Wilmington Island Oyster
    Roast," 198–201

Y

Z
Zucchini Bread 243
Zucchini Casserole, 55
Zucchini Pickles, 257

About the Author:

Native North Carolinian **Nancy Rhyne** has called coastal South Carolina home for many years. A popular storyteller and author, and much-sought-after speaker, Nancy divides her time between writing, research, and personal appearance. Her great interest in Low Country folklore keeps her on the road for weeks at a time. Through Nancy's tales, the reader becomes amazingly familiar with the beliefs, traditions, and history of the people of this unique area of the southern United States.

Nancy resides in Myrtle Beach with her husband, and traveling companion, Sid. Both are great cooks! Nancy recently attended the Johnson & Wales Culinary Institute.

Other Books by Nancy Rhyne:

Alice Flagg: *The Ghost of the Hermitage*
Carolina Seashells
Coastal Ghosts
The Jack-o'-Lantern Ghost
More Tales of the South Carolina Low Country
Once Upon a Time on a Plantation
Plantation Tales
The South Carolina Lizard Man
Tales of the South Carolina Low Country
Touring the Coastal Georgia Backroads
Touring the Coastal South Carolina Backroads

About the Cover:

Within an hour's drive of Charleston, Hilton Head Island, or Savannah, **Bonnie Doone** Plantation is located at the headwaters of the Ashepoo River, near Walterboro. An avenue of moss-festooned oaks leads to the mansion. The home's exquisitely planned interiors include gracefully carved woodwork, mantelpieces, and paneling—and a living room that *House Beautiful* magazine named one of the top one hundred most beautiful rooms in America.

Following the Yemassee Wars of 1715, with the threat of Indian warfare removed, rice planters began settling in the Low Country of Colleton and Beaufort Counties. One such planter was William Hopton, who, in 1722, received a royal land grant of fifteen thousand acres from King George I. The area quickly became the center of a thriving rice culture. Evidence of this money crop is visible today in abandoned rice fields.

The complete chain of ownership of Bonnie Doone is unclear due to the loss of many Colleton County records in the destruction of the city of Columbia during the Civil War. Maj. Henry T. Ferguson fell heir to the property and maintained it until his death in 1859, when Dr. Theodore De Hon acquired the land. During De Hon's days at Bonnie Doone, Federal troops arrived, burned the house and all outbuildings, and carried De Hon to Charleston as a prisoner of war.

No attempt was made to rebuild on the site until the early 1930s when Mr. and Mrs. A. H. Caspary of New York bought the plantation and built the Georgian mansion that stands today.

After Caspary's death in the 1940s, the plantation was owned by Peter Graves, of Graves Steamship Lines, and the Charleston Presbytery. The Charleston Baptist Association refurbished the home under the direction of designer Gloria Thiem.

The plantation is supervised by Dr. Bill Hightower, executive director of the Charleston Baptist Association, and Jack Little, a member of the Charleston Baptist Association and director of Bonnie Boone.

The plantation is utilized as a year-round Christian conference center and camp. The agenda includes an Elderhostel program. People come from around the world to attend Elderhostel and sleep in an Old South plantation manor house. Nancy Rhyne is a member of the Elderhostel faculty and lectures every month during spring and fall on the subjects "Things that Go Bump" and "A Sea Island Odyssey." Catherine Moody, Bonnie Doone dietitian, has contributed some of her favorite recipes to this book.